GUILDFORD
A Pictorial History

Front endpapers: part of *The Ichnography or Ground Plan of Guldeford, the County Town of Surrey, 1739*. Surveyed by Matthew Richardson and engraved by John Harris.

Back endpapers: part of *The South West Prospect of Guilford in Surrey, 1738*. Drawn and Engraved by John Harris.

The library in Guildford Institute, drawn by John Baker in 1981.

GUILDFORD
A Pictorial History

Shirley Corke

Phillimore

1990

Published by
PHILLIMORE & CO. LTD.
Shopwyke Hall, Chichester, Sussex

ISBN 0 85033 774 7

Printed and bound in Great Britain by
BIDDLES LTD.
Guildford, Surrey

E. M. D.
doctissimae illi feminae,
quae magis quam
quilibet alius
historiam Guildfordiensem
e tenebris in lucem
extulit, opusculum hoc
picturis exornatum,
frustra,
quod ad illam
oculis eheu captam
pertinet, indigna fortasse
sed gratissima
et devotissima
discipula
summa cum observantia
dedicat

List of Illustrations

Frontispiece: The library in Guildford Institute, drawn by John Baker in 1981

Illustration Acknowledgements

Guildford Institute: nos. 3-5, 9, 10, 16, 18, 32-36, 39, 42, 43, 46, 53, 58-64, 67, 68, 70, 72-74, 76, 81, 82, 84, 88-94, 97-99, 101-104, 106, 112, 116-120, 124a and b, 125, 127, 128, 130-136, 138, 139, 142-157, 159, 161-164, 174 and 175.

Guildford Muniment Room (Surrey Record Office): nos. 19 and 47 (courtesy of Mr. and Mrs. More Molyneux); no. 20 (courtesy of Lt. Col. Godwin-Austen); nos. 26, 40, 51, 54, 71, 79, 80 and 111 (courtesy of Guildford Borough Council); no. 37 (courtesy of the Strict Baptists, Chertsey Street); nos. 56, 57 and 65 (courtesy of the Headmaster, Royal Grammar School); nos. 66 and 69 (courtesy of the Earl of Onslow); no. 83 (courtesy of Mrs. Ruth Mansell); no. 87 (courtesy of Mrs Handa Bray); no. 129 (courtesy of Mrs. Zillah Puttock); nos. 168, 172, 173 (courtesy of Dennis Specialist Vehicles); nos. 17, 24, 38, 100, 170.

Guildford Museum: 1, 6, 12, 22, 23, 25, 29, 41, 49, 52, 75, 77, 78, 85, 86, 96, 105, 113-115, 122, 123, 126, 137, 140, 158, 165-167 and 169.

The British Library, 13; The Royal Commission on the Historical Monuments of England, 8 (Crown Copyright reserved); The National Trust, 31; private collection, 2; H. Thorp, 15, 45, 95, 109, 124c, 141 and 160; E. Clark, 27; Charterhouse School, 21, 110 and 171; Surrey Archaeological Society, 48, 50; Guildford Borough Council, 30, 55, 107 and 108; John Baker, *Frontispiece*.

Foreword and Acknowledgements

There are already in existence publications in which photographs are used to illustrate the history of 19th- and early 20th-century Guildford. Most notable are the two excellent booklets *Guildford As It Was* (1978) and *Vintage Guildford* (1981) by the Curator of Guildford Museum, Matthew Alexander, which incorporate much reliable information. Wherever possible photographs other than those in earlier publications have been reproduced in this book. Its scope is in any case rather different, since it is concerned as much with Guildford's earlier history as with the period since people started taking photographs. Geographically it has been primarily restricted to the area that was within the borough before it began to expand early this century, and there are only a few illustrations relating to the area within the extension of 1904.

Contributions to the sum of knowledge from which this book is drawn have come over a number of years from so many colleagues, friends and pupils that it is impossible to thank them all here. Those who have been particularly pestered and helpful include the staff of Guildford Muniment Room and of Surrey Record Office at County Hall, especially Jill Beck. Matthew and Mary Alexander in Guildford Museum have been unfailingly courteous and generous with information and advice, as has Mr. C. S. S. Lyon; particular thanks are due to Patricia Chapman, Librarian at the Institute, and other staff there; welcome assistance has come from John Janaway and others at the Surrey Local Studies Library; Mr. H. Thorp generously allowed access to his collections, and Mr. C. Allen, The National Trust Administrator at Clandon Park, helped with photography. During the preparation of the book Hilary Corke and Mary Stenhouse were indispensable. T. L. Zinn has contributed what only he can do so gracefully, and Stella Pickford, generous as always of her time and attention, produced perfection from a much corrected manuscript. For photography thanks are due to Eric Hunter, William Corke, Roger Smeeton, Lyn Clark and the staff of the University of Surrey's Audio Visual Aids Unit. Finally, I am grateful to the Guildford Institute of the University of Surrey for inviting me to compile this book for them, and for giving me free access to their collections, a superlative source for the history of many aspects of 19th-century Guildford. Part of this gratitude should in justice go to the band of volunteers who did so much to ensure the survival of the Institute and its material. They include Matthew Alexander, Russell Chamberlin, 'Jac' Cowie, Patricia Chapman, Janet Alderson-Smith, Mary Butts, Lyn Clark, Jill Cornell, Mary Elton, Anne Knee, Don Moore, Pam Sandison, Margaret Sellers, Dorothy Sturley, and other members of the Guildford Group of the Surrey Archaeological Society. The mistakes are my own. I thank all those mentioned in the Illustration Acknowledgements who have allowed their pictures to be reproduced in this book, and apologise if any copyright ownership exists of which I am unaware.

York House
St James's Palace
London S.W.1

When I visited the Guildford Institute of the University of Surrey in October 1988, I learned something of its story through an exhibition drawn from its own collection of notebooks, documents and pictures. A long-felt need is now answered by publishing selected items from this fascinating collection in *Guildford: A Pictorial History*.

The Guildford Mechanics' Institute, as it was originally called, was founded in 1834 and, in spite of vicissitudes, flourished until the end of the Second World War. Its membership then declined but a group of local residents, intent on preserving the Institute, sought the help of the University of Surrey. Hence in 1982 the University became the trustee of the building which now provides it with an ideal location for extra-mural educational activities. In addition, the people of Guildford continue to meet there and make use of the library and other facilities.

We are fortunate that a scholar of the distinction of Shirley Corke, formerly Archivist-in-Charge at the Guildford Muniment Room, agreed to select the illustrations and write the text of this book. As Chancellor of the University of Surrey, I welcome its publication.

H.R.H. The Duke of Kent

A Resort of Princes

The site of Guildford, where an ancient east-west trackway crosses the Wey, seems an obvious place for a settlement. Yet of Romans there is no trace and Guildford's name does not apparently much antedate Alfred. It probably describes a geographical feature: either the yellowness of the sandy ford, a spectacular interruption of the lengths of white chalk track on either side, or kingcups growing beside the river. Saxons, still unconverted to Christianity, were here in the sixth century, but we know only where they were buried, not where they lived. Probably they settled well above flood level on the east bank, on the chalk heights now Quarry Street, and just below where the Normans later built their castle. We can, however, say with assurance it was here their successors built the first church in the place that became known as Guildford.

The settlement must have grown rapidly. King Alfred owned a house there, a family rather than a Crown possession, which he bequeathed to his nephew. It is thus surprising to find Guildford replaced by Eashing in the early tenth-century list of fortified places in Wessex, the Burghal Hidage. Perhaps Guildford, overlooked by Pewley Hill and too easily accessible by water from the Thames, was not readily defensible against Danish or other attack.

There cannot have been any serious interruption in the development of what must already have been a trading place, a 'port', of some size and which may well owe its form to a reorganisation of defences in Wessex during the tenth century. This plan is essentially that shown in the *Ichnography* of 1739. Strips run back on either side of the High Street to the North and South Town Ditch. By the 18th century some expansion had taken place on all sides, especially to the east and west, where it had crossed the river, and included the castle. The original eastern boundary presumably ran up to Ram Corner and so north along the east side of Trinity Churchyard. On the west the boundary is less clear. It appears that there was little if any building between St Mary's and the bridge before the 16th century; it is therefore possible that across the High Street the borough originally ended short of Friary Street. The flood plain may well have covered all the lower, flatter part of the High Street.

The earth rampart and ditch surrounding the town were, as was the town itself in 1066, the property of the Crown. In 1274 Edward I ordered an inquisition into recent encroachments: the men of Guildford had appropriated a great part of the King's dyke surrounding the town. Neither he nor anybody else was able to stop this gradual nibbling away of the inviting open space. In 1598, when objections were raised to Thomas Parvish's blatant enclosure of part of the North Town Ditch, it appears that part of the dyke had survived into the early 16th century. Among the old people who gave evidence about the state of affairs when they were children, Robert Smallpece, aged 80, remembered as a boy falling off the bank into the ditch when a bear being baited broke loose, as did Johan Banister, also aged eighty.

In any case, by the end of the tenth century Guildford was among those burhs, or places of trade with at least rudimentary fortifications (bank and stockade), which had a moneyer and issued the national coinage. Some 80 silver pennies minted in Guildford between 975 and 1099 have been found. Minting was on a much smaller scale than at the other Surrey mint, Southwark, and seems to have involved only one moneyer at a time. However, its existence proves that Guildford had borough status at this time: the predecessors of the mayor and approved men were already running the town.

The moneyer – whose hand was to be cut off and set up on his 'mint smithy' if he struck bad money – was a person of some standing, who no doubt employed assistance. He obtained his dies from a larger mint, at one time occasionally Chichester, but latterly always London. Strict central control resulted in a coinage unsurpassed in western Europe.

Domesday Book (1086) describes a Guildford in which the King held 75 'tenements'; the sheriff held another and there were also four houses, two of which were said to be in Odo of Bayeux's manor of Bramley, a claim the county witnesses denied. The population has been estimated at about seven hundred and fifty. Presumably they all lived on the High Street. If the 81 sites are arranged along the two frontages, each occupies little more than one of the larger modern shops. The population in 1739 (over a rather larger area) was 2,754. We can assume that in the period of economic expansion before the Black Death of 1348, when Guildford was a flourishing centre of the cloth trade, it held 1,000 to 1,500 people.

There was much coming and going in the town during the Middle Ages. After the 13th century the royal palace was gradually allowed to fall down, but royal justices came to hear cases, and malefactors from all over Surrey and Sussex were imprisoned in the keep until 1488. After 1257 the County Court met every four weeks. Monks from Waltham Abbey visited their house next to Trinity Church, and monks from Waverley Abbey and friars from Newark Priory nearby visited theirs. The Dominican Friary brought a centre of learning and a school. Often the local landowners, too, had town houses.

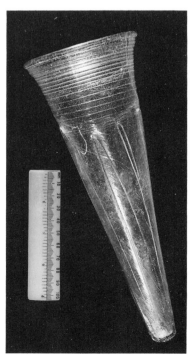

1. Amber-coloured glass beaker (4⅜ ins. x 9¼ ins.) found in the sixth-century Anglo-Saxon cemetery on Guildown (see plate 156). Thirty-six undisturbed burials of pagan men, women and children were found in the 1929 excavation. Their grave goods included beads, a spindle-whorl, brooches and buckles, as well as knives, spear-heads and pottery vessels. The finds are in Guildford Museum.

2. (i) Three silver pennies and a cut halfpenny of Edward the Confessor struck in Guildford by the moneyers Blacaman and Ælfric. Left to right: 'Sovereign/Eagles' type, EADVVERDVS REX ANGLO // + BLACENAN ON GYLDEOR. (ii) 'Pointed Helmet' type, + EDPHRDRE + // + BLACMAN ON GVLD. (iii) 'Hammer Cross' type, cut halfpenny, [+ ÆLF]RIC ON GLLD[EFOR]. (iv) 'Facing Bust' type, + EADPARD REX // + ÆLFRIC ON GILDE. Chronological order is 2, 1, 3, 4, spanning about 12 years from *c.*1052.

3. (*Left*) The late Saxon (probably about 1050) tower of St Mary's Church, the oldest building in Guildford. This view from the north shows the shallow pilaster strips characteristic of Saxon stone (or, as here, flint) work. Evidence of a smaller wooden structure found under the tower floor in 1966 must be an early, if not the first, church.

4. (*Right*) Inside St Mary's, looking from St John's Chapel through the north wall of the tower and past its south-western pier. The Norman arch has cut the bottom off a Saxon window. The tower stands on the edge of the bluff. The 12th-century chancel (perhaps the replacement of a wooden church) is three steps up, and the nave five steps down; it needed infill underneath.

5.   The rectangular stone tower keep on its mound with remains of the earlier shell keep of chalk. This photograph was taken in 1896. The castle in Guildford was one of many built by the Normans to control a conquered country. Exactly when the spur of Pewley Hill was first made into a mound, and when either keep was built, is unknown. From 1173 many payments for work are recorded.

6. The portcullised castle gate, its further flanking tower incorporated in Francis Carter's 1630 house. Henry III came frequently to Guildford. Barracks and county gaol on the motte, joined by the sheriff and his office in 1247, became an adjunct of the King's palace. This gate was built by John of Gloucester in 1256 as the castle's main entrance.

7. Henry III and his Queen, Eleanor of Provence, returning from Gascony in 1260. It was Henry and Eleanor who spent large sums improving the palace within the castle walls. In October 1274 Eleanor and her grandson Prince Henry were living there when the little boy died. His heart was buried in the newly established Dominican friary, whose members always regarded Eleanor as its 'first fundryse'.

8.   Aerial photograph of the Dominican friary during excavation, 13 June 1974. North is to the right. The entire open area is now occupied by the Friary Centre. The east end of the church is closest to the camera, and the Great Kitchen forms the north side of the cloister beyond. Structures further west were not investigated in 1974 and 1978.

9.   Undercroft on the south side of the High Street, nos. 72-74. Outside the walls of the castle was a town whose vigorous commercial life was recognised in the 1257 grant of safeguards for mercantile transactions. The only other undercroft remaining in Guildford is under the *Angel*. Used as shops or workshops, they also provided a strong dry base for the merchants' wooden houses.

10. The stone bridge at Guildford in the 18th century, upstream side. Probably of 13th-century date, the bridge of five arches was only 11 ft. 4 ins. wide. This view is before the central arch was raised in 1760 for barges to pass onto the Godalming Navigation. The ford was used until the bridge was widened in 1825. The 1900 flood destroyed this bridge.

11. Monumental brass of Sir John D'Abernon in Stoke D'Abernon church, 1277 or 1327. While the first Sir John was sheriff, ten hogsheads of stolen Normandy woad were lodged in Guildford Castle. When a further group of Normans threatened to burn the whole town, the resident under-sheriff released the woad. Subsequently Sir John had to pay the owner 120 marks, or eighty pounds.

Wool and Water

Guildford men and women were already making cloth when the Dominicans began to build their friary. In the later 14th century Francesco di Marco Datini, who founded the fortunes of Prato, was buying cloths from Guildford. Woolpacks joined the castle on the borough arms in Elizabeth I's reign and all alehouse keepers had to have one on a painted sign. There was wool from local sheep and fuller's earth not far away at Nutfield, a river to drive the fulling mills and to fill the vats there and in the dyehouses. By the end of the 16th century, though 'spinster' was still an occupation and people were describing themselves as weavers, fullers, dyers and shearmen (or finishers), most of these craftsmen were no longer independent, but 'servants' of the clothiers. Thomas Tuesley owned a large dyehouse next to the bridge, and Richard Sturt one of three in Friary Street, while Thomas Baker's and Thomas Dawborne's were below Quarry Street. Thomas Astreate's was near the corn mill and he had to be careful not 'to annoy the springs or watering place there called St Mary Wells'.

So many people were involved that the fortunes of this trade affected the whole town, though few perhaps as intimately as the shoemaker Thomas Chercher. In 1557 he took a lease of the house where the common grindstone 'for the grinding of fullers' shears' stood, and was obliged to let in everybody who wished to use it. When the demand for cloth began to decline, many people in the area – thousands, it was claimed – had no work, though in fact a limited trade continued through the 17th century. The unemployment caused concern to many people. Archbishop Abbot tried to provide alternative work, and John Parsons left money in 1702 to set up a young freeman of the town in a trade.

Guildford market, held in the High Street on Saturdays, was flourishing by 1276. By 1600 each commodity – from cattle to butter – had its defined area. Grain was at first sold under the Guildhall; a new market house projecting 15 ft. into the street had to be built in 1540. It was noted by the corporation in 1614 that profit (the corn tolls) 'was then growing by reason of the carriages through this town'. This increase, and concomitantly in other business, must to some extent have compensated for the decline of the cloth trade. For example, of the Horsnaile family living near St Mary's, John Snr. and Jnr. were beer brewer and dyer in 1657, but in 1708 John was a mealman. In 1764 the building at the end of their garden was a boulting house (for sifting flour).

It was not difficult to turn a dyehouse into a brewhouse, which happened on either side of the bridge at the bottom of the High Street. From these beginnings developed the great Guildford breweries of the 19th century: Elkins', Crooke's, Lascelles Tickner and others, and so to the Friary Brewery, itself a victim of take-over in 1974.

As 17th-century London extended its demands, a new commercial pattern began to emerge; for instance, a paper mill at Stoke. Water transport could be three to eleven times cheaper than overland. It was not until 1651 – probably prompted by Parliament's need to get gunpowder from the Chilworth mills to the Thames arsenals – that the idea of an artifical navigation, first mooted by Sir Richard Weston of Sutton Place, resulted in an Act of Parliament. This, the first major river navigation in the country, was the largest statutory commercial enterprise undertaken anywhere during the Commonwealth. Nine-and-a-quarter miles of canal were cut, and the cost, around £16,000, was far in excess of estimates and beggared many investors. Some of the frustrated subscribers considered that Major James Pitson of Stoke, who they said started life as a coverlet-weaver, had made a fortune – and ran a carriage – out of purloined money.

Certainly Richard Scotcher, whom the plausible Pitson persuaded to take over as manager of the construction when Sir Richard Weston died, by saying 'it were better his trade were in the middle of the sea than such a work as this should perish', thought Pitson a crook. Nonetheless, several of the men prominent in the town before 1662 evidently believed in the project, and lent money.

In spite of his complaints, Richard Scotcher did manage to continue his clothier's business, and paid some of the Navigation's debts to workmen in the form of cloth and blanketing. He had 'diversified' before this: in 1639 and 1640 he was involved in Archbishop Abbot's Manufacture.

After its initial difficulties the Navigation became profitable, and an advantage to Guildford, particularly by increasing the corn and timber trades.

12. St Mary's Church from the north west, by Alexander Monro, 1833. The view is from Mill Lane, below the built-up and buttressed churchyard. The houses further along Quarry Street are visible on the far side of the south aisle. The mill pool is just past the building on the right, with the waterworks beyond.

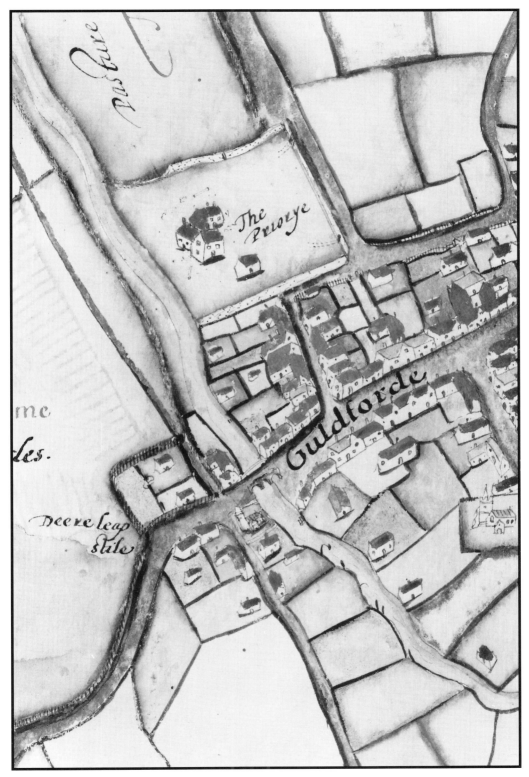

13. Part of Guildford town shown on Norden's map of Guildford Park in 1607. Buildings along the east bank of the Wey north and south of the bridge are dyehouses. The pales of the deer park run up beside the Mount and there are very few buildings across North Street. 'The Priory', surrounded by the Friars' great wall, is probably the short-lived house built by George Austen.

14. Monumental brass to Maurice and Alice Abbot, with their six sons kneeling below, in Holy Trinity Church. Maurice Abbot was a clothier. Of his sons George (4) became Archbishop of Canterbury, Robert (3) Bishop of Salisbury and Sir Maurice (5) a draper and Lord Mayor of London. Richard (1) was Master of the Hospital founded by his brother. Anthony (2) and John (6) lived and died in Guildford.

HERE LIE THE BODIES OF MAVRICE ABBOT & ALICE HIS WIFE, INHABITANTS OF THIS TOWNE OF GVILD = FORD, WHO LIVED TOGETHER MARIED 58 YEARES. & HAD 6 SONES ALL WHOME THEY LEFT ALIVE. SHEE DYED THE 15 OF SEPTEMBER 1606. BEING 80 YEERE OLD AND HE THE 25 TH OF THE SAME, MO NETH AND YEERE BEING OF AGE 86 YEERES. BOTH IN ASSVRED HOPE OF A IOYFVLL RESVRREC TION.

15. Chimneys built by Richard Burchall in 1593, at the back of what became the *White Lion*. In 1593 the clothier, Richard Burchall, just appointed bailiff, was allowed to set the sills of the frame of his new house 8 ins. further into the High Street than the old. What must have been one of the grandest houses in the High Street was the *White Lion* Inn by 1724, and was pulled down in 1956.

16. This photograph was taken by Mr. Jacobs in the 1880s, when 'an old inn in North Street was being demolished to make room for Pimms'. It could be that built by John Parvish about 1553, for which he enclosed the waste, and so provoked the earliest reference to cricket. The Bacchanalian figure in the chariot is not unusual; on the right is a hunting scene.

(manuscript document with handwritten text and merchant's marks)

17. At the Borough Court Leet, 20 January 1551, William Tomson binds himself apprentice for seven years to Thomas Baker to learn the weaver's craft. Neither master nor apprentice sign. Baker's merchant's mark is on the left, and William has made a rudimentary mark on the right. On 4 May Thomas Tomson, son of Thomas of Bookham, a shearman, executed similar indentures.

18. Thomas Baker's stoup, and the inscriptions on its base, in the Borough Plate. Thomas Baker progressed from weaver to clothier and was three times Mayor (1565, 1575 and 1580). Here again we see his merchant's mark, used perhaps proudly, since he had no difficulty in writing; his signature appears on the deed setting up Baker's school. He owned the house on the corner of Chapel Street, by the pillory.

THOMAS ✶ BAKER
1584
This ‚ Stoup ‚ new Made
1602

The Selynge for on hooll yere at thys daye endyd

Marye Aborro o	xxx	pece
Gylbarte Remnant o	ly	pece
Thomas bacar o	cccc	pece
John haman o	lxx	pece
M hyll o	ccc	pece
Harry mongar o	xx	pece
John hyllar o	cxx	pece
Nycolas penste o	lx	pece
Robarte crose o	lv	pece
M marlar o	cxx	pece
Thomas rede o	lxxx	pece
M crosly o	cxxx	pece
Robarte brodbryge o	lx	pece
Harry smethers o	xx	pece
Morys Abate o	cxxx	pece
wylliam cranly o	clx	pece
Edmonde wrigtmore o	lx	pece
Nycolas Abbcke o	cxx	pece

19. Part of a list of 32 Guildford clothiers, possibly in 1574. Most made kersey, a rough woollen cloth, in prescribed yard-wide 'pieces', 19 yards long. Both Maurice Abbot and Robert Brodbryge later got into trouble for making cloths too long, and so defrauding the crown of the 4d. duty – ulnage – due on sealing. Here Thomas Baker has made 400 pieces in the year, John A. Strete 300, and Maurice Abbot 135.

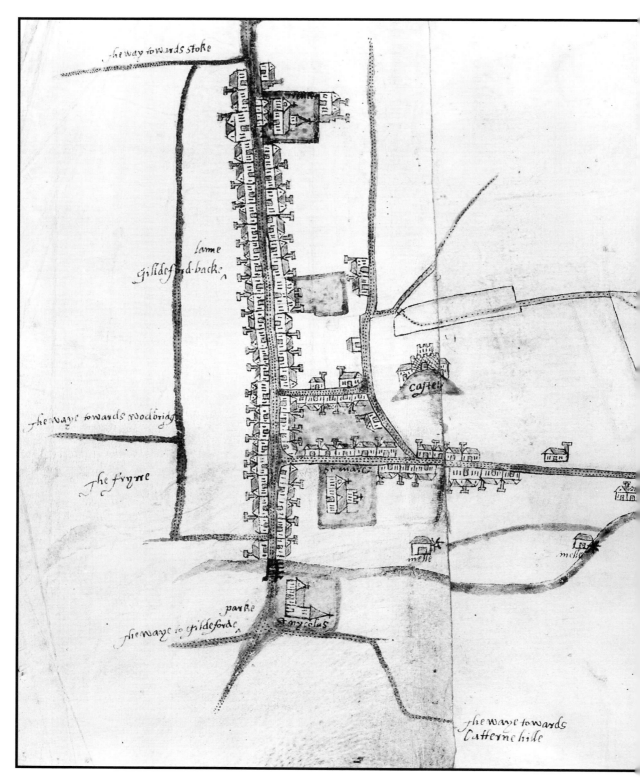

the way towards Stoke

lanne
Gildeford backe

the waye towards woodbridg

The Fryrre

Gildeford backe

Castel

St Mary

melle

melle

parke
the waye to gildeforde

St nycolas

the waye towards
Catterne hille

20. Part of a map in the early 17th-century estate book of George Austen of Shalford, showing Guildford. More schematic than Norden's map, this indicates the relative importance of different areas and buildings in the town, rather than what was actually there. The three churches, castle, the *Tun*, and the upper fulling mill and corn mill are distinguished, but not the Guildhall.

21. The backs of the Quarry Street houses upstream of the Town Mill, the ground falling away steeply to the millstream. When C. B. Phillips made this drawing in 1921 he saw gardens where earlier had been industrial buildings: dyehouses, workshops and pipe kilns. The new road constructed in the 1960s now truncates them. Some of these houses contain medieval stonework.

22. The treadwheel crane on the Wey Navigation's wharf in Friary Street shortly before it was dismantled in the early 1970s. Built soon after the town centre wharf was acquired in the 1660s, men walked inside to load and unload barge cargoes of grain, meal, coal, and bark for tanning.

23.   Rebuilding Paper Court Lock near Ripley, on one of the stretches of canal newly cut in the 17th century, May 1907. The work that went on when the 12 locks were first constructed must have looked very much like this. The upper part of the side of the lock, made of sloping turf, can be seen at the top right.

The Puritan Tradition

If there were people of Wycliffite leanings in Guildford – and it is likely – they kept out of sight. Heretics burnt in Kingston market-place in 1513 and 1540 were not from this part of Surrey. But from the middle of the 16th century onwards we know of many whose Puritan ideals of hard work, strict morality and almsgiving coloured the history of the town well into the present century.

In the 1560s and '70s the government was much perturbed by a sect founded by a Dutchman, 'H. N.', Hendrick Niclas, called 'the Family of Love'. Believers not only denied the validity of infant baptism, but also the authority of magistrates. It is curious that one of the people suspected of being associated with the 'Familists' was that pillar of late 16th-century Guildford, Thomas Baker. If not himself an adherent, he was stated to have allowed his brothers George and Harry, who were, to live for long periods in his house. No action was taken against him.

It is tempting to identify inscriptions on walls and beams in Quarry Street, in the 'Puritan' quarter of the town, with members of this and other sombre and extremist sects. At a house in Quarry Street across the road from that shown in plate 27, beams exhort readers not to 'lie, nor speak that is filthy', and to 'detest from the heart women ugly and wanton'.

Most Guildfordians who played any part in national affairs between 1550 and 1700 were Puritans. John Parkhurst, Elizabeth's first bishop of Norwich, was an accomplished Latinist and scholar, who had spent Mary's reign in exile in Zurich. His generous bequests to Guildford were to some extent frustrated because his possessions were impounded to pay for the rebuilding of the derelict Lady Chapel in his cathedral.

Archbishop Abbot was also a Puritan although, as with Parkhurst, this did not prevent his enjoying secular pleasures. In Abbot's case, his accidental shooting of a keeper when out hunting blighted his life. Another gifted scholar from the Grammar School, he was one of the translators of the King James Authorised Version of the Bible. More at home in the study than in making difficult political decisions, he was not the leader that the divided English Church needed in the years 1611-33. He paved the way for Laud, and Laud for the Civil War. Even in his devotion to Guildford, he was perhaps impractical in forcing on the town a solution – the Manufacture – which most people did not believe would work; and, of course, it failed.

During the Interregnum Guildford supported Parliament, and Puritanism could flourish unchecked. On 7 June 1644, £60 of the Manufacture money was voluntarily 'lent to Sir Richard Onslow for the use of the Parliament' (in November 1642 the Hospital had been 'forced to lend £100 to the sheriff for his Majesty's use ...'). All three parishes were among the first in the county to appoint the new official, the Register, to see to the civil registration of births, marriages and deaths. Many civil marriages were performed in the town by the magistrates, 13 before John Howe and 28 before Richard Budd. Both were members of the 1648 Surrey 'classis', and therefore presumably Presbyterians, and both were thrown out of the corporation in 1662.

Those who had been able to worship according to their Puritan inclinations before 1660 were not willing to desist. Three meeting places were licensed in 1672. Of the named men and women who were attending proscribed conventicles – assemblies 'to practise religion in another way than according to the liturgy of the Church of England' – in

Artington and St Nicholas in 1680 and 1682, some or all must have been among the '60 or 80 or sometimes 100' at a known Anabaptist conventicle in 1669. Thomas Pace, named in 1669, was their preacher on 21 August 1680. The craftsmen attending came from all three Guildford parishes, Stoke and Shalford, and included John Horsnaile, dyer, of St Mary's, Angelo Burt, a clothier, and Joseph Nettles, mealman, who in 1691 established an exhibition at Oxford or Cambridge for a freeman's son from the Grammar School.

Lady Stoughton, wife of Sir Nicholas, was present at two such meetings in 1680. In July 1683 Sir Nicholas (who had been sheriff in 1663) was fined for a meeting held at Stoughton Place, in Stoke.

Business and friendships, as always, cut across sectarian boundaries, and parish officers could be drawn from residents of any denomination. John Cooper was Surveyor of the Highways of St Mary's in 1669 as was Richard Remnant in 1674. Richard Symmes, who turned the Quakers out of Cooper's house in 1670, had been as well as a witness to it, one of the two 'loving friends' who were overseers of his father Edward Cooper's will in 1663. The other was Thomas Horsnaile.

The Onslow family's links with Guildford as Members of Parliament and High Stewards were perhaps especially close in the 17th century. In 1683, when a Puritan outburst against Roman Catholic James II was feared, and arms had been found in Arthur Onslow's house, he, his son Richard and Sir Nicholas Stoughton were indicted as being 'seditious persons ... of republican principles'. Richard Onslow was said to have stated that 'the fountain of authority is in the people and the King is accountable to them'. None of the three was punished for this attack on the Divine Right of Kings.

From the sectarian groupings of the 17th century the later Nonconformist churches developed. The chapel in Blackhorse Lane was built in 1690 by John Horsnaile. Here the Congregationalists met. The Baptists had a meeting place before 1761 and their chapel was at the end of Tunsgate. Like the Quakers, these sects declined in membership during the 18th century and then flourished, joined in the 1820s by the Methodists and in 1845 by Unitarians – though their church was not built until 1875. Many prominent Guildfordians belonged to one of these churches, and there were claims that more people attended Nonconformist worship than Anglican. When a census of numbers attending morning service was taken on Sunday 30 March 1851 there were 126 Congregationalists, 35 Particular Baptists (Tunsgate), 9 Quakers, 200 Methodists, 102 Baptists (Commercial Road), 70 at the Providence Chapel in Castle Street, and 30 Irvingites (Quarry Street). At least as many people – 164 Congregationalists – attended afternoon services.

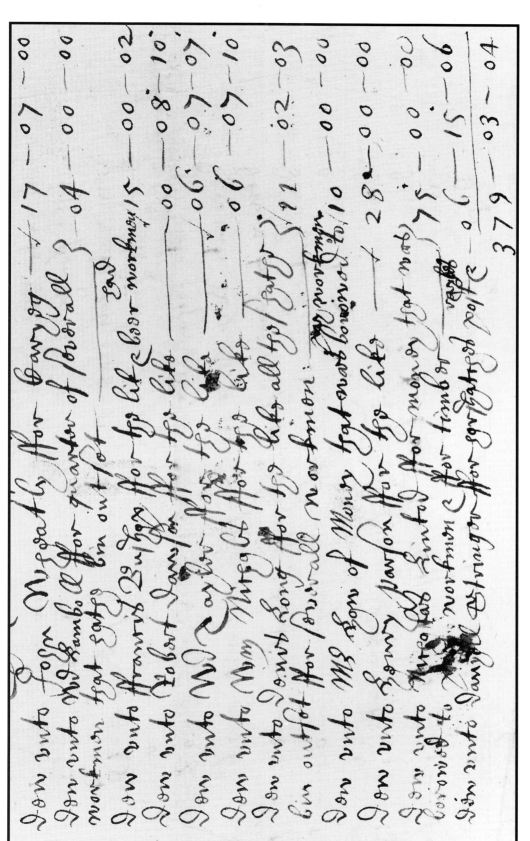

24. Some of the expenses incurred by Richard Scotcher during the construction of the Navigation, left unpaid in August 1654. Included are payments made for materials, carriage and 'quarter of severall workmen that hathe bin outset' (i.e. board and lodging). Three of the last four entries are for money borrowed from Mr. How, Henry Parson and Nicholas Lintott to pay workmen, and for timber.

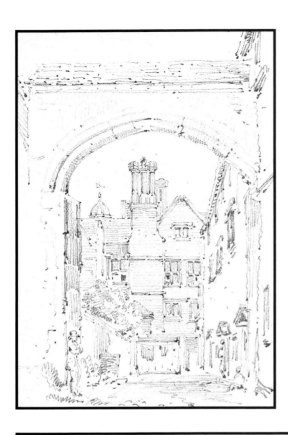

25. Looking in through the back gate of Abbot's Hospital: sketch by Alexander Monro, 1838. The buildings intended as the Manufacture are just inside on the right. His concern at unemployment when the cloth trade declined led the Archbishop to urge, from 1614, the establishment of a scheme training younger people to make linen cloth. This did not long survive its delayed initiation in 1630.

26. Extract from Guildford Borough Court Book recording the proceedings on 26 August 1662. Under the Corporation Act those who would not take 'the oaths' and the sacrament according to the Established Church were thrown off the corporation. The mayor, all six magistrates, the town clerk, eight approved men, both constables and one tithingman were replaced by 'royalists'.

27. Painted plaster on the wall of an upstairs room on the west side of Quarry Street. Dated by the clothing to the 1580s, this monochrome decoration is accompanied by pious verses:

O mortall man and wormes meate
*   remember death shall be thy eynde,*
Slack not thy tyme nor do not forgett
*   thy synfull lyfe for to amend.*

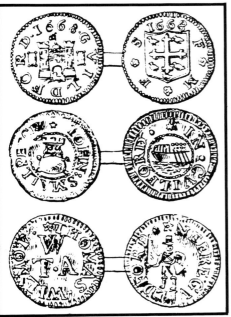

28. Trade tokens (copper coins for local circulation) issued in Guildford during the Interregnum and after. John Smallpeice shows a row barge on his token (centre), a reminder that the Wey Navigation once carried passengers and that between 1654 and 1658 both a great and a little row barge were plying on the river, earning £3 and £1 10s. a week respectively.

29.   Looking up Castle (South) Street: sketch by Alexander Monro, 31 August 1837. In 1642 Nicholas Stoughton, aged eight, was boarded 'at one Richard Scotcher's a clothier in South Street, where I went to school to one Mr. Staples and learned some of my accidence' (Latin grammar). Richard Scotcher rented a rack for drying his fulled cloth 'at the Quarry' (Rack's Close); he seems to have had Puritan sympathies.

30.   A detail of the early 17th-century mantelpiece in the Council Chamber at the Guildhall, said to have come from Stoughton Place. The carved panels represent the four Humours or Temperaments, Sanguine, Choleric, Phlegmatic and Melancholy, and are based on engravings by the Antwerp artist Marten de Vos. It would surely have been sympathetic to the melancholy – and choleric – Sir Nicholas Stoughton. In 1652 he 'had a turning to religion' and began 'to consider my sins, loved to be at digging of graves, and to look on dead men's bones'.

31. Sir Richard Onslow, 1603-64. He was J.P. 1633-62 and M.P. 1628-61. His great grandson said that he had imbibed his Puritan principles from his father, and that he was 'a very able and artful man'; Cromwell called him 'a fox with Charles Stuart in his belly' when he arrived late at the battle of Worcester. In 1660, on the other hand, he was accused of having destroyed the King's gunpowder works at Chilworth.

32. The mayor's badge and chain of gold, given by Arthur Onslow on his election as High Steward in 1673. Among the charges laid against Arthur and Richard Onslow in 1683-84 was that they had, by putting their own arms on the badge, offended against the outdated Tudor statutes of Livery and Maintenance. The badge was not used again until the Glorious Revolution of 1688.

33. The house in the High Street, one up from the Quarry Street corner and here seen in 1922 refronted and occupied by two shops, which housed the Cooper family's bakery from 1659-1750. On 3 April 1670 the 14 men attending the Quaker monthly meeting here were dragged into the street by the magistrates Richard Symmes and Henry Flutter; 'Friends sate down in the street and continued theire meeting there ... (having a stool pen ink and paper) ...'

34. 'Quakers' Acre', the burial ground next to the Library in North Street, in April 1925. The first recorded meeting of Guildford Quakers was in 1668, though births are entered from 1648. This ground, with a room for meetings at the North Street end, was acquired by John Cooper and Richard Remnant and two other trustees in 1673. The meeting house was used till 1803, and the last of many burials was in 1879.

35. The Quaker meeting house. Built mainly on part of what had been Mr. Martyr's garden, the garden of Guildford House (see front endpapers), and bought from his descendant John Martyr for £105 in 1803, a subscription for its construction raised £404 8s. The building in the foreground shows a first-floor addition to the new fire station built in 1872, the hood covering hoses hung up to dry.

36. The Congregational chapel which altered the name of Blackhorse Lane to Chapel Street. John Horsnaile is said to have built a wooden meeting house here in 1690, which was handed over to the trustees of the Congregational church by his widow in 1723. Rebuilt in 1802, the chapel became the home of a flourishing Sunday School from 1868 to 1884.

37. The Baptist chapel at the corner of Castle Street and Tunsgate in 1908. The Baptist congregation must have been one of those which obtained a licence in 1672, and had acquired this site, probably with a barn on it, before 1761. Endowments had been given by Joan Smallpeice in 1726. The chapel was rebuilt before 1842. The congregation moved to what had been the Primitive Methodist chapel in Chertsey Street in 1953.

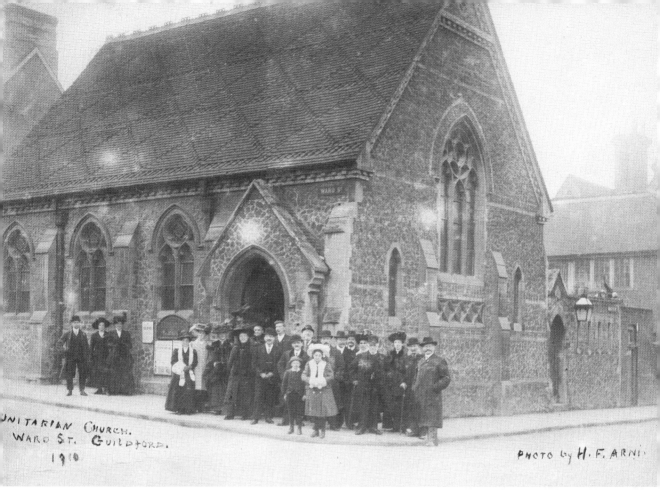

UNITARIAN CHURCH.
WARD ST. GUILDFORD.
1910

PHOTO by H. F. ARNI

38. The Guildford Unitarian church on the corner of Martyr Road and Ward Street in 1910. The congregation of this Guildford church (1875-1983) had been meeting in the long room at the *Angel* since 1845. It was an offshoot of the group established in 1699, and which settled in Meadrow, Godalming, in 1783. Mr. and Mrs. John Cooke were deeply involved in setting up this church.

39. Looking down North Street towards the end of the 19th century, a Victorian aspect which survived until the 1960s. The Methodist church erected in 1844, straight ahead, was rebuilt, larger, in 1892-4. The Congregational church, right, moved here in 1868, and added Sunday Schools in 1884. Both moved this century, the Methodists to Woodbridge Road in 1962 and the Congregationalists to Portsmouth Road in 1964.

Hogs in the High Street

Guildford in the 18th century was a small and flourishing market town. Most of the leading men, like John Martyr the solicitor who lived and carried on his business in 'Guildford House', belonged to families whose names are familiar as clothiers, brewers, butchers and so on in the preceding two centuries: Flutter, Ford, Quennell, Smallpeice, Goodyer, Chandler. Prosperity had now enabled them to call themselves gentlemen. The bookselling and printing firm of Russell produced in John Russell R.A. an artist of national renown.

Among new arrivals, professional men who chose to live in an agreeable town within a few hours of London, John Howard the surgeon is exceptional in having spent his working life in Guildford. Anthony Allen the lawyer, Mr. Pearce the London brewer, and, for that matter, the Duke of Somerset, took a limited or no part in town life. John Howard achieved unwelcome national notoriety when in 1726 he took Mary Toft of Godalming into his house to better investigate her claim to have given birth to rabbits.

The proceedings of the town Quarter Sessions set the tone in a place whose many amenities did not include elaborate sanitary arrangements. The responsibility of dealing with serious crime did not rest with the borough magistrates, who had the County Quarter Sessions and the Assizes standing behind them. In 1771 James Bylett was charged with 'stricken (Mary Eules) on the head with a porrage pott'; in 1745 the presentments of the Grand Jury included the beadle for not doing his duty with two no doubt recalcitrant hogs.

Sometimes county and borough justices worked together, as when they gave warning in 1793 that unlawful gambling at the Whitsun races on Merrow Downs would be punished; the borough justices also issued fierce notices against gambling, sabbath-breaking, swearing and drunkenness.

A case involving these last two vices and posing unwelcome problems faced them in December 1797. William Pitt was Prime Minister, Napoleon victorious in northern Italy and about to go to Egypt, and John Russell Mayor. Joseph Hockley the town clerk (whose monument is in Holy Trinity Church) wrote to the Secretary of State to ask advice. After a successful prosecution for uttering 'scandalous and seditious words', Hockley found the Treasury dilatory in reimbursing expenses. In August he was asked to send another bill, 'as in the multiplicity of papers it has been somehow mislaid'.

The expectations of its administrators may have been humdrum, but the town was increasingly busy. Guildford being 'The central or halfway Quarters between the Metropolis and Portsmouth and also between Chatham and Portsmouth', soldiers had frequently to be billeted there. In 1756 the inns could provide 210 beds and 315 stablings. A petition in 1779 that barracks might be built listed the many inns whose keepers had gone bankrupt by losing their better – and prompter-paying – customers. This had no effect, and curiously, when the government did propose to build barracks in 1794, there was an objection. An open letter in reply pointed out that it would be to the town's advantage, and that it was chiefly professional men, including Joseph Hockley, who were objecting.

Not only the innkeepers were inconvenienced. On 1 May 1757 the 21-year-old attorney William Bray, serving his articles with John Martyr, noted in his diary that Col.

Amherst's Regiment of Foot was passing through, and Mrs. Gardner had 48 horses and more than 50 men at her house, as well as attendant women and children.

Impromptu celebrations occurred. On 21 November 1756 General Blakeney arrived at the *White Hart* fresh from his heroic stand in Minorca. A bonfire and illuminations were laid on, and the mayor and magistrates went to pay their respects. William Bray turned up and had two glasses of claret. Then he joined a group of town worthies who drank the General's health from 8.00 to 10.30 p.m. The free and unchaperoned life of walks and evening visits enjoyed by the young people of both sexes, which he describes, goes far to explain the attitude of the professional parents in 1794. One bad hat of a handsome officer would have destroyed this idyll.

A constant stream of people passed through the town, some profitable to the inhabitants, some deserters, and some in need of assistance, like the 'two blacks in the street' given a shilling in 1795.

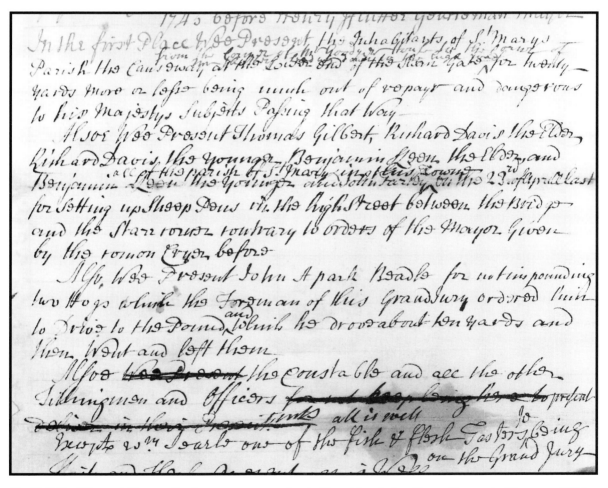

40. Guildford Borough Quarter Sessions: presentments by the Grand Jury before Henry Flutter, the Mayor, on 20 May 1745. The non-repair of a 'causeway', wrongful erection of sheep pens in the High Street, and 'John Apark Beadle for not impounding two Hogs which the foreman of this Grand Jury ordered him to drive to the pound and which he drove about 10 yards and then went and left them'.

41. The Town Bridge and lower part of the High Street, looking westwards up the Mount: drawing by John Russell, later R.A., at the age of 12 years in 1758. Star Corner is nearest on the left, and the *Swan* on the right. There is apparently no inn sign for the *White Lion*. The ford can be seen beside the bridge.

42. The lower part of the High Street before 1865, showing pens for sheep. All markets were originally in the High Street – commodities (their areas allotted in 1597) on Saturdays, animals on Tuesdays. Because it disrupted traffic the livestock market was moved to North Street in 1865, then to Woodbridge Road new market in 1895 and to Slyfield Green in the 1970s.

43. Guildford House: an early 20th-century postcard. A beautifully proportioned house, elegant without and within, built by the lawyer John Child in 1660. Behind still stands the brewhouse; its garden with banqueting house across North Street is now built over. In the middle of the 18th century it belonged to John Martyr, and William Bray lived there as an articled clerk. Later a shop and then a restaurant, it became the town's art gallery in 1959.

44. Anthony Allen's house, from the *Prospect* of 1738. In 1660 'newly built' by Thomas Canfield, this elaborately fronted house with an intricately laid-out garden behind was occupied *c.*1723-54 by a Master in Chancery who had Arthur Onslow for his patron and, a good friend to Guildford, was made a Freeman in 1726. Both *Ichnography* and *Prospect* were commissioned by him. The house was demolished in 1964.

Anthony Allen Esqr.s mansn House

45. The House of Industry behind Abbot's Hospital, 1822: a watercolour by John Hassell. This workhouse was built by subscription, apparently in 1728, and housed up to 50 paupers from all three parishes. It was sold in 1837. The *Crown Inn* later occupied the end section (left); this was pulled down in 1907. Archbishop Abbott School used the rest from 1865 and in 1891 built the existing tower.

46. Detail from a lithograph of the High Street in 1837 by E. C. Duncombe, who also worked as a surveyor. The second church of St Nicholas (1837-75) is on the right. The house just across the bridge beyond is where Thomas Tuesley's dyehouse and Mr. Charles Flutter's brewery, later Francis Skurray's, stood. The town crier is announcing an auction.

Sr Tho. Molyneux's Bill

Dec 17: 1713.

A: 1 journy to looke upon ye Knee haveing a White Swelling upon it   0 = 5 = 0

19 A: 1 journy   0 = 5 = 0

A: 1 Bottle of Balsum ye   0 = 2 = 6

28 Knee

A: makeing an Issue in ye Leg — 0 = 5 = 0

A: 3 purg's ffor horses — 0 = 3 = 0

1 = 0 = 6

Jan. 15th 1719=20

Then R. the contents of this Bill in full of all Accounts pme John Howard

47. John Howard's bill to Sir Thomas Molyneux of Loseley for attending to his knee, 1713. John Howard, surgeon and man-midwife, joined the corporation by paying a fine in 1704, and was mayor in 1747. His house was next to Anthony Allen's. His career apparently continued unaffected by the Mary Toft affair. Sir Thomas Molyneux had married Margaret More of Loseley.

48. Hogarth's engraving 'Cunicularii. A new Whim-Wham for Surrey', 4 December 1726, appeared after a week when 'every creature in town both Men and Women have been to see and feel her'. Thomas Lord Onslow, Lord Lieutenant, exposed the fraud by local enquiries which revealed that Joshua Toft, Mary's husband, had been buying rabbits too small for eating. Mary was sent to Bridewell.

Cunicularii
or
The Wise men of Godliman in Consultation
They held their Talents most Adroit
For any Mystical Exploit.

A The Dancing Master or Praeternatural Anatomy.
B An Occult Philosopher searching into the Depth of things.
C The Sooterkin Doctor Astonished.
D The Guildford Rabbit Man Midwife.
E The Rabbit getter.
F The Lady in the Straw.
G The Nurse or Rabbit Dresser.

49. Spital Street looking towards Ram Corner: sketch by Alexander Monro, 21 August 1835.
Beyond the remodelled front of Allen House on the right and what was formerly its yard, stables and
barns is the house once John Howard's. In 1734 he was permitted to extend his house two feet into
the High Street; presumably he was rebuilding. The Grammar School is on the left.

50. The Cornmarket and *Tun Inn* in 1817. The Cornmarket had moved in 1627 across the road from under the Guildhall
(which was itself rebuilt in 1683). The frontage seen here was the result of John Steere's work in 1737. Before 1835 the corn
tolls (£150 p.a. in 1820) went to the mayor, for repairs to the Guildhall and bridge, and other borough expenses.

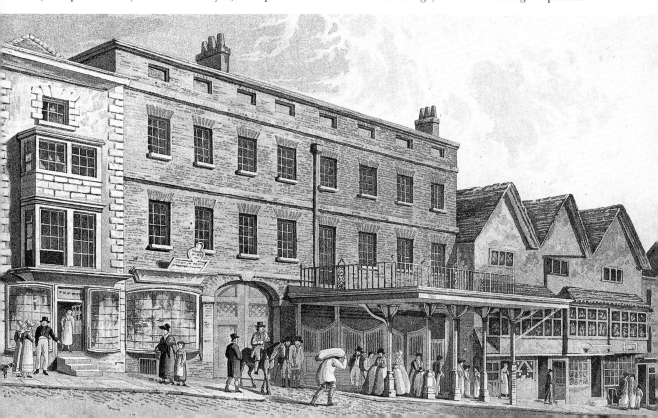

Who on her oath saith that she keeps a Publick House in the said Parish of [St] Mary's Virgin known by the Name of the Swan that on the thirtieth day of November last in the evening William Davies a journeyman Breeches maker came to her house And that she heard him say that he wished "French would invade England to morrow" and cut all the English into Mince Meat That She Examinant said to him it was a Pity but Such a Man as Men should be taken before the Mayor and made an example of Upon which the said Informant Davies said Damn and blast the Mayor and all that support him

Taken and Sworn
before us
John [Ruddell] Mayor

her
Hannah + Green
mark

John [Orundell]

51. Deposition of Mrs. Hannah Green, who keeps the *Swan* alehouse in St Mary's, as to what she heard William William Davies, a journeyman breeches maker, say on 30 November last. It was taken before two justices on 8 December 1797. First he said 'he wished the French would invade England tomorrow and cut all the English...

Inhabitants of *GUILDFORD,*

O R

BARRACKS OR NO BARRACKS.

by John Andrew Jones

A Well-Wifher of the Town of GUILDFORD offers the following Queftions to the Tradefmen and Inhabitants—

WHITHER, if the intended BARRACKS, at the FRIARY go on, they and their Families will not be very much benefited by having TWEN-TY POUNDS per Day expended in the Town, as it is computed one Regiment of Horfe alone muft expend Ten Thoufand Pounds a Year wherever they are, which Money muft circulate and find its Way into the Pockets of every Individual in the Town as well as relieve a certain Defcription of People whofe prefent Burthens are too much for them to bear. As there muft be a great many Officers in the Barracks there will be continually their Relations and Friends vifiting of them, to the great Advantage of the Inhabitants, letting their Lodgings, and the Town in General.

It is very clear there are none but profeffional men can object to a Thing fo highly beneficial to the trading Part of the Town, fuch as Attornies, the Clergy, and Medical Gentlemen, and a few Enemies to our worthy Lord Lieutenant, as it is a well known Fact, that when Soldiers are marching into or through the Town they attract the Notice of their Wives and Daughters to a fhameful Degree.

But it appears that the prefent Oppofition is not altogether whether there fhall be Barracks or not, but whether two of thofe Gentlemen fhall loofe their Fields and Gardens. But Trifles of fo private a Nature fhould always give Way to public Good.

As there will be a general Meeting at the Town Hall on Saturday, let us unite with Lord ONSLOW and Support the intended Barracks with all our Might, as a Thing of fo much Confequence to us and our Poftery was never offered before.

---

52. An anonymous reply to the 1794 petition against building barracks on the Friary estate, which had been signed by 26 people including Richard Sparkes, Joseph Pickstone, William Newland and the town clerk.

53. Detail from a mid-18th-century drawing showing the mostly unpaved High Street outside the Cornmarket and the *Tun* – here *Three Tuns* – with drain-pipes projecting far out over the street, but not as far as the multitude of inn signs.

54. Some of the resolutions reached at a meeting of the inhabitants of Guildford convened by the mayor John Martyr in the Town Hall to decide the best way to celebrate the 50th Jubilee of George III's accession, 17 October 1809. There were to be no illuminations, no fireworks or bonfires, but a subscription to 'administer comforts to the Poor People on that day'.

Resolved That on the approaching 25th day of October all Business be suspended, That the Corporation and Inhabitants of the said Town do all attend Divine Worship to return Thanks to Almighty God for the Blessings conferred on our King and Country.

Resolved That there be no Illumination, no Fire Works or Bonfires in the Town, the first of which causes a useless waste of Money (which might be applied to a much better purpose) and the whole tends to create Tumult and Disorder. —

Resolved That a Subscription be now opened and the Collection be made General throughout this Town for the purpose of administering Comforts to the Poor People on before mentioned. —

Excellent Gifts of Charity

Through the long ages before the state undertook responsibility for health, welfare and education, charity, both in its biblical sense and in that which describes its outward manifestations, was a cardinal virtue. Many people in Guildford had reason to bless those who practised it.

The name of Guildford's most famous son, Archbishop George Abbot, continues to live in the town. His hospital is the most distinguished building in the High Street and still fulfils its original purpose. Today's application of the principle it embodies, care for those who deserve well of the community they have served, has not only made possible an extension to the hospital itself, but has erected other modern imitations. The benefits of many other endowments continue to be applied to plug holes in state provision, as for example does the Poyle Charity, Henry Smith's gift in 1627. John Howe's endowment for serving-maids continues as an amusing anachronism.

The school which educated Abbot and his brothers, John Parkhurst and Arthur Onslow, the Great Speaker, continues to educate Guildford boys in the same building. To what extent the original founder of the 'free school at the town of Guildford', Robert Beckingham (1509), or those like William Hammond, and George Austen who (with financial support from local gentlemen including Sir William and Mr. George More of Loseley) saw to it that Edward VI's refounding (1552) was realised, would recognise a legitimate expression of what they worked for, is perhaps questionable. The same is true of Thomas Baker's primary school (1579) in the Rye Market House, whose funds now go to an exhibition for further education. Other projects to bring a small number of children into the ranks of the literate and numerate, such as Caleb Lovejoy's (1676) and William Haydon's (1827), have been overtaken or subsumed.

Since the National Health Act of 1946 it is easy to forget the nature of earlier provision for the care of the sick. Individual enterprise built the Royal Surrey County Hospital in 1862-66. Treatment was free (until 1928), admission being by letter of recommendation from a subscriber. Expansion and improvements – a new wing in 1887 (opened 1910), a nurses' home in 1897, and new wings in 1924 and 1925 – were mostly paid for by fund-raising campaigns. The Surrey Branch of the British Red Cross Society gave £10,000 towards the 1922 addition to the nurses' home. Much support and help were given by Sir John and Lady Jarvis, who gave £7,500 in 1927 to pay for one of the new wards. In 1934 Sir John, then the High Sheriff, wrote 'the hospital is the possession of every one of us. It is something in which the whole county should take pride'. Equally, convalescent homes and district nurses existed because of gifts and annual subscriptions.

Corporate giving is now overtaking the generosity of private individuals. An early instance of this is the Friary Brewery's rescue of Pewley Down in 1920. Other open spaces given by private citizens are Racks Close by Alderman Leonard Ellis in 1911 and the Sports Ground by Sir Harry Waechter, also in 1911. Two families may be picked out for mention. The Powell family lived latterly at Weir House. In 1897 Thomas Wilde Powell initiated a fund to keep the Grammar School in being by giving £1,000. In 1896 he was made the first Honorary Freeman, an honour extended to his grandson, Lawrence, in 1957. To provide a playing field Dr. Herbert Powell, son of T. W., gave to the Grammar School in 1914 the grounds of Allen House, and in 1926 land at Boxgrove. In 1921 he gave Henley Fort to the town. He and his sister Eleanor repaired and catalogued the

Parkhurst Library. The architect, Alderman Lawrence Powell, who sat, often as chairman, on almost every public body in Surrey, gave Millmead to the town.

To name all the benefits conferred on Guildford by successive members of the Onslow family, the largest local landowners, would make a very long list. Between 1751 and 1763 they contributed generously to the rebuilding of Trinity Church after the tower fell down. One of the few recorded generous actions of that sad recluse, the 3rd Earl, was to give the land on which the Royal Surrey County Hospital was to be built. The 4th Earl gave the land for Bridge Street and built the bridge, provided land for allotments (one of his passions), gave a recreation ground, and sympathetic assistance in the acquisition of land for sewage schemes and water supply, and made possible public access to Merrow Downs.

55. The basin and ewer bequeathed to the borough by Bishop John Parkhurst in February 1575. These fine pieces came eighth in his bequests of silver. Guildford should also have received 'a great bowl of silver and gilt with a man's head in the bottom being polled and having a long beard with the cover having at the top a naked man with a spear in his left hand and a shield in his right' and also a salt.

56. The chained library at the Royal Grammar School in 1911. All his Latin books were bequeathed to the school by Bishop Parkhurst, and 87 were received, Bishop Freake having retained some of the best for himself. In 1911 the books were kept in a room in the Usher's house. Now they are again in the gallery which was their first home.

57. Inside the courtyard of the Royal Grammar School about 1952, looking towards the Usher's house from underneath the gallery which runs across the front of the building. Originally it joined the Master's and Usher's houses, and was completed in 1586 by George Austen to accommodate Bishop Parkhurst's books. It was enlarged in 1650 using eight oaks given by Arthur Onslow.

58.   George Abbot (1562-1633), Archbishop of Canterbury 1611-33. From the Grammar School George Abbot went to Balliol College Oxford. After taking orders in 1585 he spent eight years studying theology and preaching, and became known for his strongly puritan opinions. Bishop of Coventry and Lichfield in 1609, and of London in 1610, his opposition to Charles I's arbitrary government led to his retirement from public life in 1627.

59.   Measured drawing of the cottage in St Nicholas parish said to be the birthplace of Archbishop Abbot, made by the Borough Architect and Surveyor Henry Peak in 1863, very shortly before it was pulled down. In older representations the addition on the right is a mere lean-to of boards, and the projection on the left with door and sash window had not been added.

60. Archbishop Abbot's birthplace, looking past the cottage to the entrance into Crooke's Brewery yard, close to the town bridge. This photograph, taken in 1863 just before the cottage was pulled down, shows that it backed onto the large house on Park Lane. Square in plan, it was rather larger than it looks; even so, perhaps the Abbot family moved soon after George's birth.

61. Passage inside Abbot's Hospital, 1926. Abbot had been contemplating a foundation in Guildford since 1614. The first stone of the Hospital of the Blessed Trinity was laid in 1619, and the 12 brothers and eight sisters (increased to 12 later) moved into their quarters soon after 1622. Both external brickwork and oak panelling and carving inside are of the highest quality.

62.   New Year Party in the Hospital of the Blessed Trinity, 9 January 1924. This has always been an important annual event in the lives of the inmates of Abbot's Hospital. Entry was restricted to men and women over 60, born in Guildford or resident there for 20 years. Each had his or her own rooms.

SURREY COUNTY HOSPITAL.

In Memory of H. R. H. the late Prince Consort.

As Rector of the Parish in which the County Hospital is situated, and feeling the deepest interest in its success, I would commend it to your generous support for the following, amongst other reasons.

I.   That this populous and wealthy County is as yet without any adequate provision for its sick and suffering poor.

II.   That it is an urgent duty devolving on a Christian community to endeavour to remedy this deficiency.

III.   That Guildford, the County Town of Surrey is accessible from all parts by the South Western and South Eastern Railways.

IV.   That the district of Guildford stands second in the Kingdom for its salubrity.

V.   That the site of the Hospital, which was presented by Lord Onslow, is in the most healthy part of Guildford.

VI.   That London practitioners are turning their attention to the establishment of Country Hospitals, where the purity of the air is found by experience greatly to expedite the recovery of health, after surgical operations, or bodily disease.

VII.   That a Building, capable of future enlargement if required, has been erected, which embraces every modern improvement for ventilation and other comforts.

It will contain between fifty and sixty beds, and will be completed and furnished at a cost of £15,000, of which about £11,000 is already promised.

Seven irresistible pleas are hereby presented for the generous co-operation of all who have the means to help this benevolent work.

Those who enjoy good health may regard this as a most favourable occasion for a grateful thank-offering to Almighty God for the greatest of earthly blessings, and those who are afflicted with infirmity may well be anxious to contribute, out of sympathy to fellow sufferers.

T. GOODWIN HATCHARD,
Rural Dean.
Rector of St. Nicholas, Guildford.

September, 1864.

[TURN OVER.

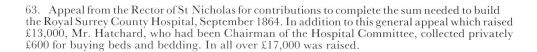

63.   Appeal from the Rector of St Nicholas for contributions to complete the sum needed to build the Royal Surrey County Hospital, September 1864. In addition to this general appeal which raised £13,000, Mr. Hatchard, who had been Chairman of the Hospital Committee, collected privately £600 for buying beds and bedding. In all over £17,000 was raised.

64. The Royal Surrey County Hospital soon after completion in 1866. Edward Lower, a Guildford architect, won the competition and the foundation stone was laid on 31 July 1863. There were 60 beds, and 248 in-patients during 1867. The medical staff comprised one resident house surgeon, three honorary medical officers and three honorary assistant medical officers.

VICTORIAN CONVALESCENT HOME

FOR SURREY WOMEN.

SURREY HOUSE, BOGNOR.

LONDON OFFICE : **39**, Victoria Street, Westminster, S.W.

W. T. CUNNINGHAM, Asst. Sec.

REGULATIONS
TO BE OBSERVED BY

PATIENTS IN THE HOME,

who shall, whilst they remain in the Home, pay strict attention to them.

PATIENTS ARE ONLY RECEIVED ON THURSDAYS, and may proceed to the Home by any Train,
but SHOULD ARRIVE at the HOME NOT LATER THAN 5 p.m.

All insured persons are required to bring with them their MEDICAL CARD.

1.—*No patient shall on any pretence whatever enter a public house, or purchase or partake of any alcoholic liquors outside the Home.*

2.—The patients shall pay their own fare to and from the Home, and shall come in clean clothing and provided with a change of linen, including night dress, slippers without nails or brads in heels or soles, strong shoes for exercise, and brush and comb; all linen must be marked with the surname of the patient. A change of clothes is advisable. On entering the Home the patients shall deliver up their parcels.

3.—Patients shall rise when the bell rings, and not earlier without permission. They shall retire to bed directly after prayers, and half an hour later all lights shall be extinguished and no talking allowed.

4.—Unless excused, the patients shall attend daily morning and evening prayers, to be conducted by the Matron in the Home.

5.—The patients shall be punctual to meals at the time appointed.

THIS PAPER IS TO BE KEPT BY THE PATIENT, AND NOT RETURNED TO THE OFFICE.

6.—Patients shall make themselves useful in such ways as the Matron shall direct.

7.—When the weather permits, the patients may (unless forbidden by the Matron) leave the Home for recreation.

8.—On quitting the Home for the purpose of recreation, the patients shall leave the sitting-rooms in order; work, books, papers, &c., being neatly laid aside, and no patient is to enter the sitting-room in out-door shoes.

9.—All medicines, ointments, etc., to be given to the Matron.

10.—All hats, bonnets, coats, jackets, shoes, &c., of the patients shall be kept in the appointed places.

11.—The patients while within doors shall keep to the rooms set apart for them and shall not enter the kitchen or offices except by instruction of the Matron

12.—No gaming, raffling, swearing, or immoral conversation shall be permitted among the patients, upon pain of dismissal from the Home.

13.—The patients shall keep their clothes in the lockers or other places provided for them, and shall on no account leave them about the rooms or on their beds, and they shall not wash any of their apparel in the Home; but, when required, shall place such apparel where directed, so that it may be washed at the laundry.

14.—The patients shall not return to their bedrooms during the day, without the permission of the Matron.

15.—All the patients while resident in the Home are required to comply with the orders of the Matron, who shall have full power to dismiss any inmate guilty of misconduct or disregard of regulations.

16.—The patients, when aggrieved, may complain to the Matron, or to the Committee, or to the appointed Visitors, if any.

17.—No patient is allowed to bathe in the sea without the permission of the Matron and Medical Officer, or go in a boat, steamer or yacht, without asking permission of the Matron.

18.—No intoxicating liquors shall be consumed on the premises unless the use thereof shall have been sanctioned by the Matron under the direction of the Medical Officer.

19.—The Committee cannot be responsible for money or valuables belonging to patients, unless they are given into the charge of the Matron.

No large boxes must be brought to the Home.

65. Rules of the Victorian Convalescent Home for Surrey Women in Bognor, *c.*1912. This home, opened in commemoration of Queen Victoria's Diamond Jubilee, took Surrey women from several hospitals. The Guildford representative in 1914 was William Shawcross. These rules come from Lord Onslow's papers. A subscriber, he would have recommended patients.

66. The opening of the George Shepherd Prentis and Emilie Prentis Convalescent Home in Worthing, 18 June 1909. G. S. Prentis, a Guildford chemist who had retired to Keymer, gave £10,000 to build and endow the home. It housed 10 patients from the Royal Surrey County Hospital, and filled a long-felt need. Designed by E. L. Lunn, it was opened by Lady Midleton and closed in 1939.

67. William Hillier, 4th Earl of Onslow. Born in 1853 and an only child, he succeeded to his great uncle's desolate house at Clandon in 1870. A man of great energy, his busy political life culminated in four years as Governor of New Zealand, and coincided with a period of agricultural depression. He sold building land north and east of Guildford.

68. Hillier's Almshouses, formerly on the Farnham Road just above the Royal Surrey County Hospital, c.1885. The 4th Earl took his second name from his grandmother Susannah Hillier, one of the daughters and co-heiresses of Nathaniel Hillier, a printer, who lived at Stoke Park. In 1880 Lord Onslow presented land whereby these almshouses, established in Shoreditch by the Hilliers, could move to Guildford. Accommodation was provided for 12 inmates.

69. Letter from Louisa Dodgson to the 5th Earl of Onslow, 1920. Louisa and Henrietta, the last surviving sisters of Charles Dodgson, better known as Lewis Carroll, left the Chestnuts, their family home since 1868, in 1919. Louisa is evidently hoping to get a servant into Hillier's Almshouses, which received poor women more than 45 years old, Anglican or Dissenters.

Nutley
York Rd - Guildford
May 4. 1920

Miss L Dodgson is not sure whether Lord Onslow has been told of the change of address of Miss Emma P. Poole, whose name Lord Onslow kindly put down for one of the Hillier's almshouses - Farnham Road Guildford — she is still in Miss L. Dodgson's service, but they have left The Chestnuts + are now living at "Nutley" York Road - Guildford —
they moved last July —

70. Lawrence Powell (1889-1973). Buildings designed by Lawrence Powell include Compton Village Hall, but much of his time was devoted to voluntary public work. He was particularly interested in music and the arts, and was involved in the establishment of the first public library in Guildford. He designed the bronze doors in the south transept of the cathedral.

The Burden of Progress

As in the wider world, an increasing population brought environmental and other problems. The old structures of borough government were seen to be inadequate, here as elsewhere. The Municipal Reform Act of 1835 created an elected borough council with wider powers and ever more numerous statutory obligations. The better-off – the voters – did not always welcome change. They tended both to accuse the council of not doing anything to redress what was wrong, and to complain of extravagance if action was taken. All too often the resolution in response to requests or petitions was that 'no action be taken in the matter'. To let well alone was a conscious or unconscious principle: 'in view of the fact that the present scheme has hitherto worked satisfactorily they do not consider it advisable to amend it' (1913).

Nonetheless, innovations there were. The first statutory improvement had been made in 1760. Under the 1759 Act for Watching and Lighting Guildford two watchmen were to go their rounds every hour through the night, crying the hour and the weather. Routes were defined, beginning at the Guildhall and in one case returning to it 'down the Milkwoman's Gate'. Petitions often collected hundreds of signatures. Around 1814 the Mayor and 800 inhabitants begged Parliament not to introduce a 'Bill to regulate the importation of Corn'.

Not until 18 years after the first public meeting urging it was an act for Paving, Cleansing and otherwise Improving the town passed in 1812, and new commissioners appointed. A pamphlet (1849) pointed out the harmful and cholera-producing effect the dreadful sanitary conditions in Guildford – 'the open mouth of a sewer disgorging its filth' into the Wey on one side of the town bridge – had on the overcrowded poorer inhabitants. The last cholera epidemic was in 1866. A Local Board since 1864, in 1872 Guildford complied with the provisions of the 1866 Sanitary Act, made itself an Urban Sanitary Authority, and set to work. The town had already in 1857 and 1866 taken over the 1701 Water Undertaking, and (1857) been given powers in the Guildford Gas Light and Coke Company, which was established in 1824.

Improvements followed apace: better scavenging (1895), new and deeper wells (1871 and 1926), a public bath and wash house (1889, following a petition in 1850), a sewage system (1889-95), an enlarged Borough Police Force (1836-1946) and Fire Brigade (1863-1947). Many of these borough undertakings later fell victim to the post-Second World War rush of rationalisation and nationalisation, and left borough control, as also did education in 1945.

At the turn of the century two groups hitherto excluded from power, working men and women of all classes, joined forces. The Trades and Labour Council asked that the Education Committee might include a member of the working classes, which came about in December 1903. From 1913-18 they shared premises with the suffragettes (many the wives and daughters of leaders of the local community). In 1920 the Guildford branches of the Women's Co-operative Guild and the Independent Labour Party both wrote to the town council with suggestions about the future utilisation of Day Nursery premises. Although Guildford has never elected a Labour M.P., and is now regarded as one of the least likely places in the country to do so, the Labour Movement got off to a brave start under the aegis of the veteran socialist Edward Carpenter, who ended his life in June 1929 at 25 Mountside Road. The first Labour candidate stood in the 1918 election.

71. Handbill announcing the opening of a market in the old cockpit, October 1800. The octagonal cockpit at the back of the yard of the recently bankrupt *Red Lion* is on the *Ichnography* (front endpaper). The eastern part of the yard had been made into a public highway, Market Street, with a theatre and Assize Court built on its western side.

72. Demolition in 1925 of the first reservoir at the foot of Pewley Hill. A larger reservoir was constructed immediately above in 1853 for new houses (Charlotteville). This one, constructed by William Yarnold in 1701, was too low to supply them with water by gravity. River water had first been pumped to it from the mills up hollowed elm pipes, but after 1860 the water came from a spring. Both these first two reservoirs were roofed in 1886.

A MARKET eſtabliſhed at GUILDFORD, for BUTTER, EGGS, POULTRY, &c. &c. every *Wedneſday* and *Saturday*; in the Building, formerly occupied as a

COCK-PIT,

now furniſhed with SEATS, STANDS, WEIGHTS and SCALES, &c. for the Accommodation and Shelter of both Buyers and Sellers: The Market-Hours are from NINE to TWELVE on *Wedneſdays*, and from NINE to ONE on *Saturdays*.

Ruſſells Guildford, Printers.
October 13th, 1800.

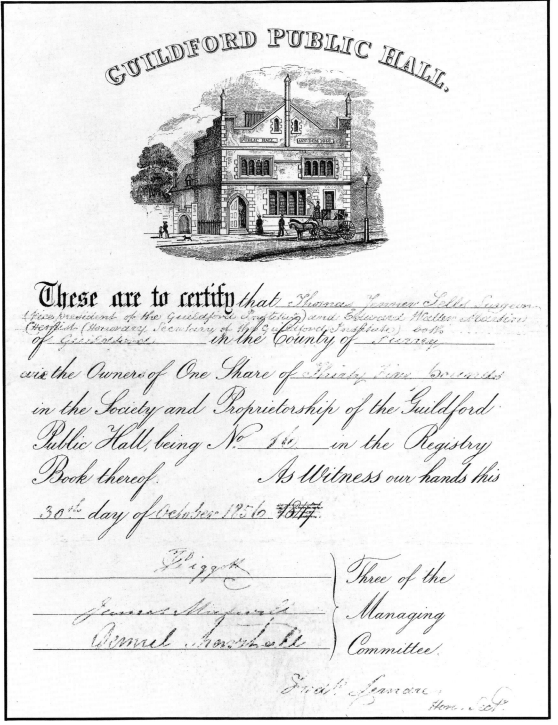

GUILDFORD PUBLIC HALL.

These are to certify that *Thomas Inman Sells Surgeon (Vice president of the Guildford Institute) and Edward Walter Martin (Chemist (Honorary Secretary of the Guildford Institute) both of Guildford* in the County of *Surrey* are the Owners of One Share of *Thirty Five Pounds* in the Society and Proprietorship of the Guildford Public Hall, being No. *16* in the Registry Book thereof. As Witness our hands this *30th* day of *October 1856* ~~1877~~

Piggott

James Marshall

Daniel Thornthell

} Three of the Managing Committee.

Fredk. Jenman
Hon. Sec.

---

73.   Share no. 16 in the first Public Hall in North Street, erected in 1846. The hall was the first purpose-built place of assembly, close to the corner of Leapale Lane. This £35 share was presumably held by the officers in whose names it was issued on behalf of the Institute, whose home was here from 1846-92. Dr. Sells was the builder of Charlotteville.

74. Laying granite setts in the High Street, 1868. On the right in a top hat is the bearded Henry Peak. He was the first Borough Surveyor (1864-91) and an architect who designed very many buildings in various styles, including Smallpeice and Merriman's near Tunsgate. He was responsible for the infrastructure and much of the superstructure of early 20th-century Guildford. Going uphill from the post office (H. R. Copus), the business premises comprise E. Drewett, photographer; W. Stevens, poulterer and fishmonger; Williamsons, upholsterers; Alfred Lemare, professor of music.

75. The Cornmarket as rebuilt in 1818. On the left is the passageway up the Tuns Gate; the two arches, behind the paved open space where the corn sacks were brought for bargains to be struck and tolls collected, lead into the new court room for the Assizes.

76. The large hall in the County and Borough Halls, fitted up as the Assize Court, c.1880. The Assizes moved here from Tunsgate in 1861. Eighty feet long, this hall could house 1,000 people. In 1912 it was converted into the Theatre Royal.

GRAND GALA DAY

Opening of the West Surrey

LUNAT(I)IC CITY POLICE STATION

The Model Refuge and Tramp Association

Lodging House Company (unlimited), beg to announce that no expense will be spared to make the above a **Grand Success**. £9,000 has already been expended to give éclat to the occasion. The

ANTI-RATEPAYERS

WILL INVITE

LORD BURY DE CASH

On Horseback, to head the procession, and after receiving an illuminated address will call on

MAJOR GREENHORN

TO INTRODUCE

THE MAYOR AND CORPORATION

To explain their wisdom and foresight in building

Peeler Mansion

And urge them, regardless of cost, to adopt all Modern Appliances for the comfort of their lodgers, efficient Cooking and Warming Apparatus, and **Electric Lighting**, with Hot and Cold Baths always ready

THE RATEPAYERS' ASSOCIATION

Will be there in full force with Bands and Flying Colours, to hear the City Architect's new Laughing Song—"Jolly Dog" a la Jolly Nash. A Deputation of the Corporate Verbosity Society will then join in the jovial Chorus led by

LORD DUNDERHEAD ON A DONKEY,

Who will Address the Meeting and ask the

Local Government Board

What use they are going to make of

PEELER MANSION

And fix the opening Day. It is expected the Market Committee will take a back seat and look on at their New Corn Exchange and give up the Old One for a Green Market. It is thought Ratepayers will

COME IN THOUSANDS

Publicans and Shop-keepers will simply be told to **Shut-up** but may obtain permission to look on at the Rateable Spectacle and torture-you-light proceeding.

By Order,

JUBILEE JUBILANTE,

Hon. Sec.

Skit Lodge, Madhouse Lane,
June, 1983.

P.S.—There is no **GAMMON** about this, somebody's House came down with a run and the Ratepayers run it up again sharp; good business this—particulars at 6970, Peeler Mansion Buildings.

G. 3516

77. Handbill satirising the new Borough Police Station in North Street, opened in 1893. More suitable accommodation than that behind the Tunsgate court room was designed by William Lower, with underground access to the court room in the Guildhall. Its cost of £9,000 was resented by some ratepayers, hence this lampoon. The façade still exists.

78.   Installing sewage pipes under the Wey in Stoke, *c.*1906. This pipe carried sewage to the new sewage works at Bellfields. The second stage of Guildford drainage cost £53,000, and provided the borough with an up-to-the-minute system. This pipe can be seen on the 1906 plan opposite.

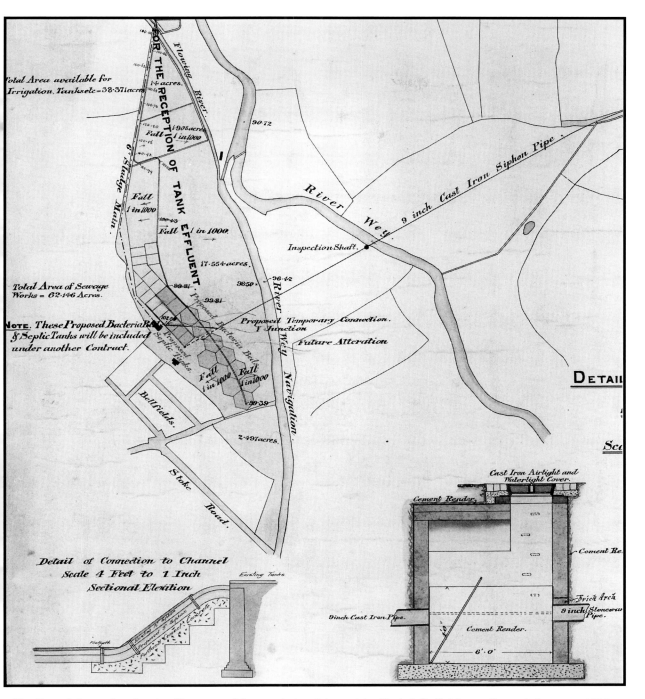

Total Area available for
Irrigation, Tanks etc = 38·37 acres.

FOR THE RECEPTION OF TANK EFFLUENT

Flowing River

14 acres.

1·908 acres.
Fall 1 in 1000

Fall 1 in 1000

Fall 1 in 1000

6" Sludge Main

Total Area of Sewage
Works = 62·146 Acres.

NOTE. These Proposed Bacterial
& Septic Tanks will be included
under another Contract.

Proposed Bacteria Beds

Proposed Septic Tanks

17·554 acres.

98·50   96·42

99·81

99·81

105·56

Fall 1 in 1000   Fall 1 in 1000

99·39

2·49 acres.

Bellfields.

Stoke Road.

River Wey

River Wey Navigation.

90·72

9 inch Cast Iron Siphon Pipe

Inspection Shaft.

Proposed Temporary Connection.
Y Junction
Future Alteration

DETAIL

Sc

Detail of Connection to Channel
Scale 4 Feet to 1 Inch
Sectional Elevation

Existing Tanks.

Footpath

Cast Iron Airtight and
Watertight Cover.

Cement Render.

Cement Re.

Brick Arch

9 inch Stoneware Pipe.

9 inch Cast Iron Pipe.

Cement Render.

6' 0"

79.   Part of a large plan showing 'Sewerage of the remainder of the parish of Stoke', C. G. Mason, Borough Surveyor, 1906.
This system ran from the top of Warren Road, downhill across the Epsom and London Roads, serving streets not yet
wholly built up, to the sewage works at Bellfields. This area was not included in the town drainage scheme of 1889-95. The
section is of the 'Screening Chamber and Catch Pit'.

Alternative Elevations.

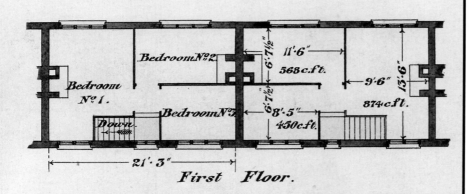

Bedroom Nº2.

11'·6"

6'·7½"

563 c.ft.

9'·6"

13'·6"

Bedroom
Nº 1.

6'·7½"

Bedroom Nº3.

874 c.ft.

8'·5"

Down

450 c.ft.

21'·3"

First Floor.

Design with through

Ventilation.

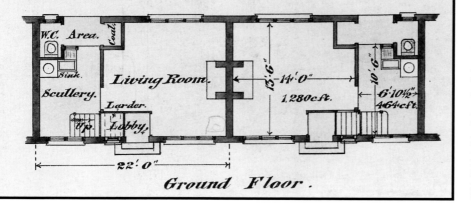

W.C. Area.

Coal.

Sink.

Living Room.

15'·6"

14'·0"

10'·6"

Scullery.

1.280 c.ft.

6'·10½"

Larder.

464 c.ft.

Up.

Lobby.

22'·0"

Ground Floor.

80. 'Proposed Houses for
the Working Classes. Block
of Four Cottages'.
C. G. Mason, Borough
Surveyor, 27 and 29 April
1911. Detail from a sheet of
plans of two and three
bedroom houses, to be built
in Woking and Old Farm
Roads at Slyfield Green. The
first two blocks were started
in July 1911. The borough's
first 'tenements' had been
built in Cline Road in 1905.

81. The Suffrage Shop, in the High Street from 18 May 1913 until 1919. Guildford Women's Suffrage Society was started in February 1910. The Guildford Trades and Labour Council held its meetings here from 1913-18; at one in August 1917 it was proposed that a district branch of the Labour Party should be established.

82. Women's Suffrage: afternoon assembly in North Street, 27 July 1913. In connection with the Suffrage Pilgrimage to London, meetings were held in North Street in the afternoon and evening. The evening gathering was reckoned to be the largest public meeting ever held in Guildford, around 8,000 people attending. There was much barracking, and after Miss Dorothy Hunter's half-hour speech the police closed the meeting for fear of riot. The speakers' waggonette had been nearly overturned, and suffrage literature was trampled underfoot.

83. Miss Dorothy Hunter (1881-1977), probably about 1903. Dorothy was the daughter of the solicitor Sir Robert Hunter, co-founder of the National Trust. Through him she became a friend of Millicent Fawcett, and travelled round the country between 1904 and 1910, addressing groups of largely working-class women with great success. She was known as 'The girl orator' and her speeches are said to have contributed to the 1906 Liberal victory in the Guildford Division. She devoted her later years to the National Trust, and Haslemere affairs.

The Railway Effect

The railway from London reached Woking – or rather the station in the middle of a heathy waste round which a new town was to develop – in 1838. For seven years a procession of horse-drawn taxis, or flies, carried passengers to and fro between here and Guildford, along a narrow muddy road. The London and South Western Railway was extended to Guildford in 1845, continued to Godalming in 1849, and to Portsmouth in 1859. In 1849 also the Reading, Guildford and Reigate Railway connected Guildford westwards via Reading with Oxford, the West and the Midlands and to the east via Redhill and Tonbridge with channel resorts and ports. In 1869 a line to Horsham opened, and in 1885 the route to London through Effingham Junction and Surbiton provided a second station for commuters in the eastern part of the town. 'Guildford has become a great central point of railway communication.'

Guildford had always been an attractive place in beautiful countryside. Cobbett had found the town 'the most agreeable and most happy-looking that I ever saw in my life', not long before the railways made it so conveniently accessible. Many classes of people could and did now choose to live or stay there: professionals working in London, those retiring from a lifetime abroad, younger people looking for jobs, reasonably prosperous people taking their large families for holidays. To meet their needs, houses were built, for sale or leasing, roads, sewers and water pipes installed, and a multitude of other necessities of civilised life soon followed: schools, a hospital, a theatre, clubs, libraries, orchestras, entertainment of all kinds. Guildford expanded in many senses. The old ways of a country town were replaced by an essentially commercial society serving the middle class. Markets were pushed to the outskirts of the town. Both its aspect and its nature changed. The picturesque and small scale were swept away together with the unhygienic.

Lewis Carroll and his friends provide good examples of the draw of Guildford, at a junction of railways. Lewis Carroll would surely never have thought of a Guildford home for his sisters and younger brothers in 1868 had it not been for the line from Reading, which meant that he could even travel from his rooms in Christ Church, Oxford, to the Chestnuts and back within a day. He could also use the Chestnuts as a base for the evening visits to London theatres which were a favourite recreation. In the summer the seaside of the Isle of Wight and Eastbourne was within easy reach for himself and his sisters. One of the first friends he made in Guildford, W. W. Follett Synge, retiring early from the diplomatic service, had just come to live in a large house off the Woodbridge Road. Later Frederick Hale Puckle came back from Australia and also settled in Woodbridge Road. His daughter, Louisa, whose efforts when attending Lewis Carroll's logic lectures in Abbot's Hospital made the logician urge his sister Louisa to 'get Miss Puckle to cure herself of her morbid love of truth', went on to become a member of Guildford Education Committee, as did Roger Fry's sister Joan. Several clerical friends settled for shorter or longer periods in Guildford. Dora Abdy, the first pupil of Guildford High School to attend Oxford University, had been brought to Guildford by her mother (who went to live in Sydney Road) in order that she and her sisters might attend this recently (1888) founded school.

The railway brought change in many other ways, one of them being that after 1849 no more coaches passed regularly up and down the High Street. This affected the coaching inns; unfortunately for them there was a gap before the motor car arrived.

Whereas in the 18th century many new arrivals in Guildford were established professionals, in the 19th there was an influx of up-and-coming young men, often of humble origins, with ideas and ambitions. A number of the successful firms in the years on either side of 1900 were established by them. George Lissant Jacobs, the coach builder, came from Taunton; Robert Salsbury, the watchmaker, from Pershore; William Shawcross, the photographer, from near Manchester; Joseph Billing, the printer, from London 'via Woking'; and John Dennis, the motor manufacturer, from near Bideford. All must have had their first view of the town from the railway station.

84. Toll-gate on the Portsmouth Road south of Guildford: looking north, shortly before 1870, when the road left the control of the 1748 Turnpike Trust, and was taken over by the Highway Board. Tolls had fallen sharply as soon as the Guildford to Portsmouth railway opened in 1859; the last coach from London ran in 1849. The crippled gate-keeper is John Turner.

85. Early 19th-century tradecards of Guildford inns. The great inns on the High Street, the *White Lion*, the *White Hart*, the *Angel*, the *Crown*, and the *Red Lion*, had existed to serve the Portsmouth traffic and they benefited from the long-distance coaches. Some, however, never recovered from the billeting of soldiers, and found it difficult to survive in a railway world.

86. The yard of the *White Hart Hotel*, 1833, by Alexander Munro. The *White Hart* at the top of the High Street had the largest and grandest rooms of any Guildford inn, and many public functions took place here, including the County Ball. During the Assizes, when the Bar Mess was held in the Assembly Rooms, 100 to 200 people often sat down; here also was the headquarters of the Tory Party. The inn, which was built no later than the 17th century, was pulled down in 1905.

87. William Bray's overnight bill at the *White Hart*, 1818. At this time he had finished the *History of Surrey*, was living partly in Shere, and was still working in his London office and as steward of some Surrey manors. He has added the tips he paid. The inn, run by the Bonner family from 1838 to 1905, had been rescued by a tontine, 1803-1838, after going bankrupt.

88.   Millmead House in the 1860s. Built by William Haydon in the 1740s, it was occupied by the banking family until 1816, and then leased, often to soldiers. Lieutenant General Sir Patrick Craigie in the 1860s was followed in the 1870s by Captain W. B. O'Connell. In 1892 the Simpsons, old friends of Lewis Carroll's, were there. The house is now part of the Borough Offices.

89.   New houses in Woodbridge Road, *c.*1870. Guildford was advertised as 'The most beautiful town in the south' and houses of all sizes were built to meet demand. These are not as grand as those on the west side of Woodbridge Road; there were small semis and artisans' dwellings to the west of the river and further east in Stoke.

90.   North Street in the 1870s. The fire station, built in 1872 and later increased in height, is now the public convenience on the corner of Ward Street. The old house beyond, where the Institute is now, was among the first here; possibly it was Robert Abbot's house in 1598. Next is Henry Peak's *Surrey Arms*. Near the 'Reformers' Tree' orators, including suffragettes, later held forth.

91.   Guildford in the 1890s.   This view, from near the bottom of Fort Road, looks down on the southern half of Quarry Street, with the mill and Filmer and Mason's foundry beyond. Behind the tower of the third church of St Nicholas (1872) is Guildford Park Farm, with new houses on Lord Onslow's building estate between its fields and the Farnham Road.

92. The Tumbling Bay at Mill Mead in the 1880s, looking across the houses at the bottom of Quarry Street to the hill where Abbot Road now climbs up to Warwick's Bench. The Great Quarry can be seen on the right. This is the site of the upper fulling mill in the early 17th century.

93. The view downstream from the Town Bridge in the 1860s. On the left is Crooke's Brewery, on the right two coal wharves, and beyond a barge moored beside the Wey Navigation's treadwheel crane. Water transport could not compete with the railways. An experimental comparison in 1907 by Lord Farrer and William Killick found a ton of coal from a Nottinghamshire pit cost 25s. by barge and 22s. 7d. by rail.

94. Lord Crewe unveiling the memorial plaque to Lewis Carroll designed by Mr. Graily Hewitt, in the presence of the Mayor, Mr. William Harvey, 24 May 1933. Several members of the Dodgson family were there. Paid for by performances of *Alice* during the centenary year of his birth in 1832, the plaque was placed on a gatepost of the Chestnuts, where he died on 14 January 1898. He is buried on the Mount.

Merchants Round the Table

In the 19th century the landed gentry – often themselves not long settled in their rural seats – looked down on 'trade'. Secure in financial success and proud of their good works, the families who ran the Guildford industries and businesses were not worried by the opinions of their customers. They built themselves large houses on the London or Epsom or Warren roads, or in the villages close to the town; paid to send their daughters to the High School or one of its predecessors, and, when serving a turn as Mayor, held their own with royalty or local nobility.

This did not mean that they were always friends. A love match between the members of the Congregational Jacobs and Gammon families looked like becoming a Montague and Capulet affair, but happily had a conventional resolution.

In the carrying out of what they considered their obligations to the town these men and women were punctilious and devoted, if at times unimaginative. They served on the town council and its committees, always aware that expenditure on however worthy an object would mean higher rates, and this was something their electorate would fight against. The expense involved in two necessary projects in 1868, pitching the High Street and purchasing the waterworks, left the town with a debt of £28,000, though the waterworks made a profit of £2,500 to £3,000 a year. As the town grew larger, financial problems were eased.

The Committees and Boards of Trustees of other elective and voluntary bodies benefited from their members' business skills, among them School Boards, Burial Boards, Abbot's Hospital, the Poyle Charity and other Guildford charities, the Grammar School, Archbishop Abbott School, the Royal Surrey County Hospital and, in due course, Surrey County Council. Maurice Lacy, who joined the Board of Billing's in 1897 wrote 'from 1901 I was mad on housing', and he published a pamphlet 'No Room to Live in Guildford'. Under the chairmanship of the Strict Baptist Joseph Billing and his sons Joseph and Robert, the firm improved matters: in 1906 the Paxton Cottage Scheme completed 24 houses and, in 1926, 36 more followed on the Woodbridge Hill Gardens Estate. At least one town councillor, Mr. Triggs Turner, was one of a select band of males who supported the Suffragettes. When they held a stormy meeting in the town in May 1908 he invited two of the speakers, Mrs. Hicks and Miss Matters, to dinner. Maurice Lacy's sympathies did not unfortunately extend to the Suffragettes. He was president of the Anti-Suffrage Society, and said in 1913 that the country did not want votes for women. They might get into Parliament, and even into the Cabinet. 'The idea of a woman presiding over the Army, Navy, and Home Office or Local Government Board was absurd.'

A particularly notable philanthropic undertaking which achieved national fame was Mayor Harvey's Work Fund, whereby donations paid the unemployed to build the Lido open-air swimming bath in 1933.

Many of these busy men – and their permanent officials, like the solicitors John Rand Capron, Clerk of the Peace and Coroner, and F. F. Smallpeice, a long-standing Town Clerk – were members of Guildford Institute. Other members included Dodsworth Haydon, W. P. Trench (of Haydon's Bank), Robert Salsbury, W. T. Patrick, Edward Waller Martin, and H. A. Powell. Some of them gave talks, as did G. C. Jacobs on the Antipodes and Australasia in 1908.

95. Filmer and Mason's 'Guildford Improved Plough', *c.*1860. Edward Day Filmer, ironmonger at 84-6 High Street (home to an ironmonger since 1737), was one of the liberals on the pre-reform corporation who was not re-elected in 1836. The foundry, established about 1794, was at its most prosperous in the 1860s and '70s, making all kinds of agricultural equipment, including water wheels for Clandon Park and Paddington Mill, Abinger. The Mill Mead works were demolished in 1941. Booker's Tower is in the background of this advertisement.

By Special Appointment to H.R.H. Duke Alfred of Saxe-Coburg-Gotha,

ESTABLISHED A.D. 1800.

MAY & JACOBS

GUILDFORD and GODALMING.

ONLY THE BEST WORK.   AT COMPETITIVE CHARGES.

96. Advertisement of May and Jacobs, coachbuilders, *c.*1895. Three generations of the Jacobs family developed this business, started by William Watson in 1800, in Spital Street, on a site which later housed the Municipal Offices. Their carriages were sold to royalty, and throughout the British Isles and abroad. When cars replaced carriages, the firm became a garage, closing in 1928.

97. Haydon's Bank in the High Street, before 1883. William Haydon started to add banking to his business as a draper in the middle of the 18th century, and by the end of the century this house was known as a bank. A family concern until 1883 when taken over by the Capital and Counties Bank, it has been a branch of Lloyds since 1927.

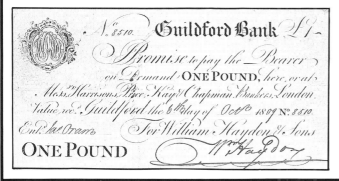

98. Bank notes of two of Guildford's early 19th-century banks, 1809 and 1838. The Guildford Bank of William Sparkes and Anthony Lee came to an abrupt end in October 1840 when Mr. Sparkes, once known as 'the King of Guildford', went straight from chairing an agricultural dinner to drown himself in the Wey. The bank went into liquidation and Samuel Haydon took the vacant place on the council. Another bank belonged to the Mangles family; the Savings Bank was started in 1816.

99. Dodsworth Haydon, who died 17 September 1901, aged 71. It was on his retirement that Haydon's Bank was taken over. Like many other members of his family he was active in Guildford life, being for many years a Councillor, Mayor in 1869, a magistrate and chairman of the Constituency Conservative party. He was closely involved in the purchase of the waterworks. A genial and popular figure, he shared with his distinguished neighbour Lewis Carroll a taste for illustrated nonsense and amateur dramatics. He also drew cartoons.

100. (*Below* and *below left*) Mr. and Mrs. John Cooke. John Cooke ran a provision merchants' shop in the High Street. He was prominent in the affairs of Guildford Institute. Treasurer of the Unitarian Church appeal, he and his wife ensured its building in 1875.

LIST OF MAYORS, 1770—1897.

1770   James Shrubb .... Solicitor
1773   Edmund Elkins .... Basket Maker
1774   Thomas Jackman .... Benefactor to Abbot's Hospital
Portrait now there
1779   John Russell .... Printer (now Stents')
1785   Matthew Wise .... Baker
1786   John Ford .... Gentleman
1787   John Peché .... Surveyor General of Windows
1788   Joseph Pickstone .... Attorney (now County Club)
1789 T John Russell .... Printer and Cutler
1790 T Richard Sparkes .... Draper and Banker
1791 T John Russell .... Printer and Cutler
1792 T John Martyr .... Attorney (Bull's Shop)
1793   John Arundell .... Baker
1794   Joseph Pickstone .... Attorney-at-Law
1795   James Vincent .... Grocer (Gate's Shop)
1796   John Peché .... Surveyor General of Windows
1797 T John Russell .... Printer & Cutler (now Stents')
1798 W Charles Booker .... Corn Merchant and Miller
Town Mills
1799 T Richard Sparkes .... Draper & Banker, Bank House
1800 T John Nealds .... Innkeeper
"Vintner's Arms" now Nealds & Cooper.
1800 T Richard Sparkes .... Banker
1801 T John Nealds .... Innkeeper
1802 T John Martyr .... Attorney
1803   James Vincent .... Grocer
1804   Robert Harrison .... Baker (Reynard's Shop)
1805 T Samuel Russell............. Printer and Cutler
1806 W George Waugh .... Draper(Colebrook's Fish Shop)
1807 W Charles Booker .... Miller and Mealman
1808 T John Nealds .... Brewer "Vintner's Arms" Tap

1809 T John Martyr .... Attorney, High Street
(Martyr Road named after him)
1810   John French .... Draper and Banker
(Sparkes' Partner)
1811   Joseph Hockley .... Solicitor
(Pickstone's Partner) afterwards Town Clerk
1812   John Tickner.............. Maltster (subsequentlyFreakes)
adjoining " Horse and Groom" North Street
1813 T John Nealds .... Maltster and Brewer
1814 W Charles Booker .... Miller and Corn Merchant
1815 W George Waugh .... Draper
1816 T William Elkins............. Grocer
1817 T John Martyr .... Attorney
1818 T Joseph Haydon............. Draper and Banker
(Dodsworth's Uncle)
1819   John Nealds .... Malster, Brewer, & Innholder
1820   ,, ... *(now Hodgson's)*
1821 C William Sparkes .. .. Banker
1822 C John French .... Banker
1823 L Charles Booker .... Miller, Town Mills
now Waterworks
1824 C William Elkins .... Brewer, Bear Lane
now Friary Street
" Billy whip, Billy bung, from a Basket Maker sprung—to a Grocer he was bound, then got Mayor of Guildford Town." (Last Mayor to sentence a culprit to be whipped at the cart tail.)
1825 C James Stedman............. Surgeon *(late Dr. Stedman's father)*
1826 C William Sparkes .... Banker, &c.
1827 C John Rand .... Solicitor
1828 L George Waugh .... Draper
1829 C Joseph Haydon .... Banker
1830 C William Elkins .... Brewer, Bear Lane
1831 L Charles Booker............. Corn Merchant, Quarry Street
(Built Booker's Folly.)

1832 C James Stedman .... Surgeon
1833 C William Sparkes .... Banker & Coach Proprietor
1834 C John Rand .... Solicitor
1835 C   ,,   ,,
1836 C John Smallpeice, on Jan.1st after passing of the Municipal Corporation Act .. Solicitor
1836 C Anthony Lee, on and after Nov. 9th .... Banker
1837 C Joseph Haydon .... Banker
(William Sparkes' Partner)
1838 C William Sparkes .... Banker & Coach Proprietor
Horsed Coaches from Guildford to London, ran "Royal Blue" Coach to London, opposed L. & S.W.R. main line via Guildford to Southampton, called 'King of Guildford,' subsequently committed suicide by drowning above the Tumbling Bay after Presiding at the Guildford Agricultural Dinner.

T Tory.   W Whig.

1839 C James Stedman .... Surgeon *(Horncastle)*
1840 C James Haydon ...... Banker
1841 C William E. Elkins .. Brewer
1842 C Joseph Weale ...... Draper
1843 C Casteels Cooper .... Oil and Colorman *now Shillingfords*
1844 C William King ...... Grocer corner Chapel St. *now Clark's*
1845 C Joseph Haydon ...... Banker
1846 C Thomas Jenner Sells . Surgeon
1847 C Joseph Weale .... Draper
1848 C   ,, ... ,,
(now Pratt's)
1849 C John Ryde Cooke .. Provision Merchant
First year the Mayor was paid a Salary, viz: Sixty Guineas. First Corporation Flag worked by his wife, now in the Council Chamber.

L Liberal.   C Conservative.

YOURS FAITHFULLY **W. R. EMERY.**

1850 C Samuel Haydon .... Banker
Originator of Wesleyan Church in Barrack Field
1851 C Thomas Jenner Sells .... Surgeon
1852 C William Taylor.............. Butcher (now Stubington's)
1853 C Joseph Weale .... Draper
1854 C John Ryde Cooke .... Provision Merchant
now Stephenson's
1855 C William E. Elkins .... Brewer "Vintner's Arms" Tap
1856 C Samuel Haydon .... Banker
1857 C William Edmund Elkins...... Brewer, North Street
1858 C Henry Piper .... Gun Maker
1859 C   ,,   ,, ... ,, *(now Gill & Carling's)*
1860 C John Palmer .... Timber Merchant (now Moons)
originally kept the "Greyhound" Inn
1861 C William Edmund Elkins...... Brewer
1862 C Henry Piper .... Gunsmith
1863 C Philip Whittington Jacob .. Surgeon and Linguist
1864 C   ,,   ,,   ,, ... ,,   ,,
1865 C   ,,   ,,   ,, ... ,,   ,,
1866 C   ,,   ,, ... ,,
During this Mayoralty the 5th of November Riots were suppressed, and the Water Works purchased by the Corporation.
1867 C E. T. Upperton .... Yeoman
1868 C   ,,   ,, ...
1869 C Dodsworth Haydon .... Banker
now Capital and Counties Bank
1870 C Edward T. Upperton .... Yeoman
1871 C Hoffgaard Shoobridge .... Draper
1872 C William Triggs .... Watchmaker, &c.
1873 C   ,,   ,, ...
1874 C Edward T. Upperton .... Yeoman

1875 L Philip William Lovett........ Solicitor, Bank House
1876 C William Triggs .... Gold and Silversmith
1877 C Frederick Augustine Crooke .. Brewer and Maltster
1878 C Frederick Thomas Lethbridge . Coal Merchant & Barge Owner
1879 C   ,,   ,,
1880 C Edward T. Upperton .... Yeoman, Wilderness Farm
1881 C William Triggs.............. Jeweller
1882 C   ,,   ,, ... ,,
1883 C Edward Thomas Upperton.... Yeoman
1884 C John Mason ... . Builder
1885 C   ,,   ,, ...
1886 C William Swayne .... Builder
1887 C   ,,   (Our good Queen Victoria's Jubilee)
1888 L Thomas Stephenson........ Provision Merchant
1889 L   ,,   ,, ... ,,
1890 C William Wells ..... Farmer and Brickmaker
1891 C   ,,   ,, ... ,,
1892 C William Swayne .... Builder
1893 L George Tayler .... Barrister
This year Mayor's salary raised to £105.
1894 L Robert Salsbury .... Watchmaker, etc.
1895 L   ,,   ,, ...
During this Mayoralty the Borough Banking Account transferred from Capital and Counties to London and County Bank!
1896 L Christopher Wrist .... Grocer and Pork Butcher
1897 L   ,,   ,, ... ,,   ,,
1898
1899
1900

Printed and Published by W. Stent & Sons, 82, High Street, Guildford.

101. Part of W. R. Emery's election leaflet, in the 1898 Municipal Election. The main reasons for his standing were 'Firstly as a protest against the ineptitude of our Corporate Body; secondly ... to assist the Ratepayers in a reasonable desire to stem the torrent of waste'. A councillor since 1893, he was re-elected on this occasion. He was an auctioneer and house-agent by profession and objected to the nature of the council.

102. The Duke of Connaught at Guildford Station, 2 June 1894. The Mayor, Robert Salsbury, is short and bearded and standing under the clock. Also present are the sergeant-at-mace, Thomas Hooke, holding the large mace given by the 6th Duke of Norfolk in 1663, the town crier, W. Tilbury, town councillors and visiting mayors. The Duke was attending the Southern Counties Agricultural Show in Shalford Park.

103. Candidates about to dice for the Maid's Money in 1911, in the Council Chamber, where this event still takes place each January. John Howe's charity (1674), together with John Parsons' (1702), provide what is now pocket-money for two of a dying breed, the domestic servant. Present on this occasion are left to right: W. Williamson, W. Boughton, C. Holden, W. Swayne, Mr. Barlow, the solicitor and secretary to the trustees, G. J. Jacobs, H. T. Gill, W. Stevens, W. R. Carling, A. Hart, Mr. Clark, Mr. Moon, E. L. Lunn, and T. G. Swayne.

104. William Swayne, builder. This William Swayne was the son of the William who started a building firm in Guildford in the 1840s. Working to a high standard, and often used by the Guildford architect Henry Woodyer, they built many houses, schools and churches, and rebuilt St Martha's Chapel. The family had been farming at Hall Place, Merrow, since the early 18th century.

106. (*Facing page*) Testimonial from the employees of Guildford Gas Light and Coke Co. to F. F. Smallpeice, 19 July 1927. The gas works (established 1824) moved eastwards across the river in 1853. F. F. Smallpeice, of an ancient Guildford family, was town clerk from 1875 to 1902, and was involved in everything that went on in Guildford. He gave the new Museum Gallery in 1911 and was behind the building of the Muniment Room.

105. (*Below*) Dapdune Wharf soon after 1909, with the barge *Dapdune*, built there by G. and A. Edwards, employees of William Stevens, and launched in 1909. Dapdune was the first wharf acquired by the Wey Navigation; gunpowder was then stored here. Later it was 'the timber wharf'. The Stevens family, who at the end of 150 years owned the whole Navigation as well as running their own barge firm, had started as lock-keepers. Harry Stevens gave the Wey Navigation to the National Trust in 1963.

EIGHTY·FOURTH·Birthday.
We·would·like·at·the·
same·time·to·express·our·
appreciation·of·your·kindness·
towards·us·in·various·ways.
We·all·sincerely·hope·that·
you·may·long·be·spared·to·
continue·as·Chairman·of·
the·Company.
With·best·wishes·for·
your·continued·good·health.
·JULY·19ᵗʰ·1927·

The Guildford Gas Light & Coke Company
1843 1927
To ALDERMAN
FERDINAND SMALLPEICE JP
We·the·employees·of·the·
Guildford·Gas·Light·&·Coke·Coy
viz·Office·Works·&·Distri-
buting·Staffs·desire·to·offer·
you·our·hearty·congratulations·
on·the·attainment·of·your·

Pomp and Circumstance

Guildford's importance was determined by geography and the Norman kings who built the castle. Fifteen royal charters and grants established it. Known to have been a borough and to have had a Guild Merchant before 1257, the second charter of that year made it the home of the county court and the county town of Surrey. From this the right to pay the town's dues directly into the Exchequer (1366), incorporation (1488) and a separate Commission of the Peace (1603) followed, as did Parliamentary representation. Not only was Guildford a Parliamentary Borough, returning two members to Parliament between 1295 and 1885 (one only during the Commonwealth and 1867-80), but elections of County members also took place there, as they do today for the constituency called Guildford. Proclamations were and are made in county towns, though the only occasion now is on the succession of a new monarch. This is still the duty of the High Sheriff of Surrey in Guildford. The monarchs themselves were not infrequent visitors before the Georges.

When the judges of the High Court came to Surrey on their regular visits, the 'Assizes', to hear the most serious cases they usually came to Guildford. These solemn occasions involved the provision of a suitable court room, lodgings for the judges, and hospitality to all those involved, from prisoners (needing a secure gaol) through a host of officials up to the High Sheriff himself and his Javelin men. At first the Assizes took place in the court room in the Guildhall, as did the Borough Quarter Sessions and other courts until the building of the new courts in 1986. In 1788 Lord Grantley erected a new building for the courts in the part of Red Lion Yard that was being made into a road, Market Street. This was superseded in 1818 with the building of the new cornmarket, with a court room at the back. The judges complained of noise, and in 1861 moved to the large hall in the County and Borough Halls. A condition of the conversion of this hall into the Theatre Royal in 1912 was that the smaller hall to the east should be enlarged and made convenient for the Assizes. A judge later complained that the balloons left floating on the ceiling here by the previous night's revelry were an unsuitable decoration for a trial for murder.

By now, well accustomed to the twice-yearly paraphernalia of the Assizes, the borough saw any attempt at moving them elsewhere as a threat to its status. In the 1920s attempts were made to find a site for a suitable building: the site of Allen House, or at the end of the Tunsgate, were suggested. All to no avail. From 1930 all Surrey sessions of the Assizes were to be held in Kingston-upon-Thames, since 1889 the home of County Hall. Proclamations, trials and elections all brought crowds into Guildford, and the town had its share of noisy, even riotous, occasions. Before the days of a secret ballot and universal suffrage, elections were occasions for lively campaigning, often vivid insults and generous gifts, not yet classed as bribery. Between the headquarters of the Tories in the *White Hart* and the Whigs across the road at the *Crown* sometimes more than words passed. It was a small world. Those voters who thought he had let them down by forming 'an alliance ... with the Irish Demagogue O'Connell' assured James Mangles in 1835 that he had 'an intimate knowledge, not only of your constituency, but of almost every Inhabitant in the Town'. He lived at Woodbridge.

107. Impression of the late 16th-century borough seal with the Latin legend 'Seal of the Borough and Town of Guildford'. Although the borough had been entitled to a common seal since 1488, this beautiful silver seal is the earliest to survive. Sixteenth-century impressions of an earlier seal are known. Many towns with a royal castle used the castle on their arms; Guildford at some date unknown added the royal arms, woolpacks, lion, key and other details.

108. The silver head of the Mayor's logwood staff, 4 ft. 4 ins. long. The inscription says 'Fayre God Do Justice/Love thy Brether'. There is a tradition that it was given by Queen Elizabeth I, although there is no record of her being in Guildford in 1565. Thomas Baker was Mayor for the last three months of this year.

109. The Court Room in the Guildhall looking north: an anonymous drawing, before 1788. In 1589 the Guildhall was 'enlarged and made longer in the north end and the Queen's Armes and the Armes of the Town set in the window'. When this drawing was made the room had a ceiling, and was ready for the Assizes.

110. The Court Room in the Guildhall looking south, 1922. The timbers of the 1589 roof are now exposed. The panelling is of the same period as the 1683 frontage, which included John Aylward's clock. Borough Courts were held here till November 1986. The Guildhall is presumed not to have moved from its original site, and there is medieval work in the building.

111.   Queen Elizabeth I decorating the initial capital letter of her name in a copy of the 1563 Act of Parliament which confirmed the Grammar School's right to rents from the lands given as an endowment by Robert Beckingham. George Austen copied the document into his history of the school, and probably made the drawing himself, early in the 17th century.

112. (*Right*) James Mangles, 1762-1838, M.P. The son 'of a ship-chandler at Wapping', he and his brother managed a successful shipping firm, many of the voyages being to Western Australia. About 1800 he moved to 'a cottage' at Woodbridge, and was High Sheriff in 1808. In 1829 he handed over his shipping interests to his son, bought the Wanborough estate, and then stood as Liberal candidate for Guildford. In 1837, aged 74, he was successfully operated on for a cataract. He had 12 children. His daughter Ellen married (on her 16th birthday) James Stirling, founder of Western Australia.

113. (*Below*) James Mangles offers a dinner ticket to those who voted for him in 1835. This kind of 'bribery' was not abolished by the 1832 Reform Act. As voting was not yet secret, and a list of votes was published, it was easy to tell who was entitled to this largesse.

MR. MANGLES respectfully requests those of his worthy Friends, who may be disposed to celebrate his return to Parliament by their own fire sides as on the last occasion to send the inclosed Dinner Ticket, on or before THURSDAY the 2d of APRIL next, to his Agent MR. G. S. SMALLPEICE who will in exchange for such Ticket, give the Bearer thereof an Order for

> TWELVE POUNDS OF BEEF,
> ONE GALLON OF STRONG BEER,
> TWO QUARTERN LOAVES,
> THREE POUNDS AND A HALF OF FLOUR,
> TWO POUNDS OF SUET,
> TWO POUNDS OF RAISINS,
> ONE POUND OF CURRANTS,
> AND
> TWO BOTTLES OF WINE, (PORT OR SHERRY).

MR. MANGLES also begs respectfully to inform those Friends who may not feel disposed to dine in public, and may not wish themselves to exchange the Dinner Ticket, that the same is transferrable to any of their Neighbors.

An Answer is respectfully requested to be sent to MR. G. S. SMALLPEICE, on or before THURSDAY the 2nd of APRIL next.

---

114. & 115. (*Facing page*) There were three candidates for the two Guildford borough seats in the 1837 election: James Mangles and Charles Baring Wall, who had won the last two contests, and Major Scarlett. Mangles and Wall were local; Scarlett came from Lancashire, though his lawyer brother had been created Lord Abinger (where he lived) in 1834. Mangles had had printed copies of a memorial in April 1835 signed by 55 voters, which accused him of voting contrary to his election pledges, together with his reply a few days later defending his actions and saying that he would not resign since he had received another address signed by three times as many voters and approving his 'Upright, Conscientious and Independent Votes'. These fly-sheets ventilate the issues of two years earlier. Mangles lost his seat to Scarlett.

To the ELECTORS

OF THE BOROUGH OF

GUILDFORD.

BROTHER ELECTORS,

Have you forgotten that Mr. MANGLES (over anxious to shew his zeal in respect of the NEW POOR LAW), stated in the House of Commons, that the new System worked well in this Neighbourhood, and that the Poor were generally satisfied with it; whereas, it had been in operation but *for so short a time*, that it was impossible for any one *even to guess* what the effect would be, and the Poor were complaining loudly of the hardships they were exposed to?

I appeal to you as Husbands--Fathers--Brothers-- Sons. Will you sanction such conduct, by your Votes?

I appeal to you as TRADESMEN. Will you, by your Votes sanction a Law, that every day's experience tells you is the Destruction of Trade?

I appeal to you as PROTESTANTS, (whether of the Established Church, or Dissenters of any denomination). Will you vote for a Man who, *on all occasions*, supported O'CONNELL and the *Popish Faction?*

I appeal to you as INHABITANTS OF THIS BOROUGH. Will you vote for a Man who is, at all times, ready to promote the Interests of *Godalming*, even to the prejudice of this Town?

I appeal to the FREEMEN, and SONS of FREEMEN. Will you vote for a Man who voted for your disfranchisement.

Lastly, I ask you, Have you forgotten the *notorious Barrack-Field Job*, and the Parties concerned in it?

I am Your well wisher,

AN ELECTOR.

GUILDFORD, July 19th, 1837.

ELECTORS

OF

GUILDFORD

You have not forgotten that the Duke of Wellington, Sir Robert Peel, and the Tories voted for the Poor Law Bill.

Ask Mr. SCARLETT if he will vote for the *repeal* of it.

Who contributed £100 towards rebuilding Saint Nicholas Church in Guildford?

Mr. MANGLES.

Who spends an immense income in this Borough?

Mr. MANGLES.

Who is the benefactor of the Poor, and the generous supporter and kind hearted friend of all who want assistance and advice?

Mr. MANGLES.

Who supported the Act which gives £10 Householders the right to vote?

Mr. MANGLES.

Who opposed that right?

Mr. Scarlett's Father.

Where does Mr. SCARLETT live? Would you ever see him, except when he comes to ask favors at your hands?

Persevere in your INDEPENDENCE, and the ELECTION is YOURS.

An Elector.

(LUCY, PRINTER.)

BROTHER ELECTORS,

The party who wished to dictate the return of TWO Members now cringe for your support.—They find you will not allow your Borough to be locked up.

116.   This vase, presented to James Mangles by the 'Reformers of Guildford' after he lost the 1837 election, shows that there was a strong body of reforming Liberal opinion in Guildford, even though it had not been able to prevent the rejection of Mangles. The voting was Wall 252, Scarlett 188, Mangles 159.

117.   Probably the declaration of the poll at the general election, 1935. The successful candidate for the south-west or Guildford Division of Surrey was Sir John Jarvis (Conservative), who sat till 1950. He initiated the Surrey scheme to help the distressed areas of Jarrow, and started five new industries on Tyneside. Lady Jarvis provided the Jarvis Maternity Home in Guildford.

118. Proclamation of the accession of George V on 11 May 1910 from the steps in front of Holy Trinity Church, by the High Sheriff, Harry Waechter. Sometimes the proclamation was read from the Guildhall balcony. Harry Waechter, who lived at Ramsnest, Chiddingfold, was High Steward of the borough between 1911 and 1922.

119.   Lifeboat Day in Guildford, 21 September 1904. The procession with the lifeboat, drawn by six horses and proceeding stern first, had already been up the High Street earlier, when the crowd was smaller.

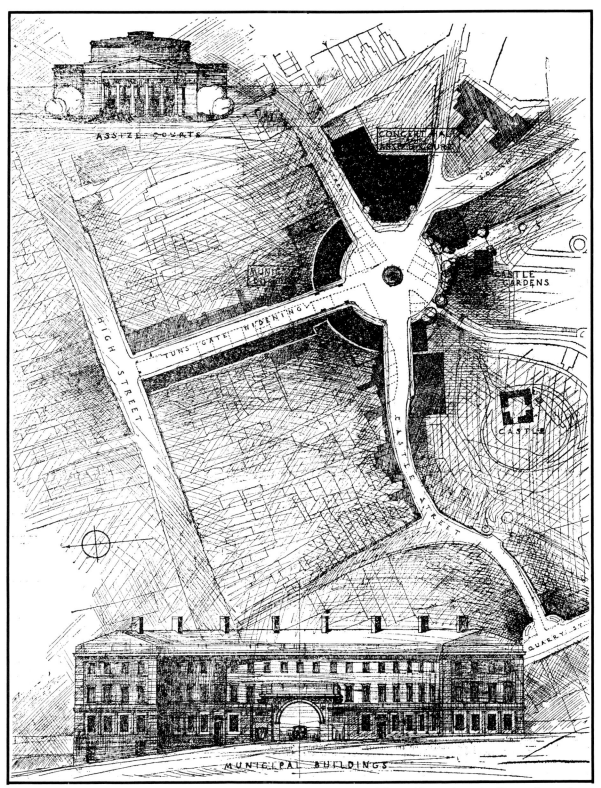

120.　A grandiose plan to keep the Assizes in Guildford, 14 January 1928. The architects Annesley Brownrigg and Hiscock propose a 'Place' 150 ft. wide, with semi-circular municipal offices pierced by an arch spanning a 40-ft. wide Tunsgate on the north, and Assize Courts and a concert hall to the east. Traffic would proceed up a widened Castle Street and down Tunsgate.

"The Right Path of a Virtuous and Noble Education"

Guildford, like any ancient town, has always been a home of schooling. Since the days of the Blackfriars this has obviously been so; but merchants would have needed the skills of writing and casting accounts before 1274. Most teachers since Milton's time would have subscribed to his description (above) of what their life's work was about. Among their number are all concerned with Thomas Baker's School, the Royal Grammar School, Archbishop Abbott School, the Guildford Infant School, all the elementary schools established during the 19th century by national religious bodies and parishes, and doubtless also many masters and mistresses who taught in their own parlours and kitchens.

The fortunes of schools always rise and fall according to the talents of their heads; in the past this could mean, as with the Grammar School in 1765, an empty schoolroom. Unendowed schools often died with their founders. Some of the numerous 18th- and 19th-century private day and boarding schools for boys and for girls in Guildford have left no trace at all. Mrs. Green identified and provided details about many of them (*Some of the Schools of Guildford. Sidelights on Guildford History III*, 1954).

Private instruction in the 17th century is even harder to document. Often clergymen took one or more private pupils. In 1675 Nicholas Stoughton sent his son Lawrence to board with Mr. Burscough 'our Minister of Stoke'. Here the boy learnt some Latin. In 1676 he was moved to board with Mr. Noble, 'a writing master who lived in Stoke', where there were about 20 young boys; a Mr. Perkins was to teach him. Fifteen years or so earlier, in a phrase uncomplimentary to Dame Schools, Mrs. James Pitson was said by one of her husband's detractors, who was trying to establish that he was 'a very meane inconsiderable person', to have been 'a teacher of litle children to reade ...'

Guildford has an interesting record in education outside schools and beyond school-leaving ages. There were non-Anglican Sunday Schools teaching basic skills as well as Bible Study. In 1852 the 'Gratuitous Evening School' began teaching boys and girls who could not go to school by day. Robert Macdonald, a draughtsman and electrician, ran an evening Mission School in various places in the town for nearly forty years, teaching reading and writing to the youngest pupils. In the last years before his death in 1899 he was helped by volunteers who gave what might be called technical instruction in their crafts.

The part played by Guildford Institute – or Institutes, for it included the Mechanics' Institute, and a second schism was healed in 1892 – in adult education cannot be overestimated. The stimulus and value of a library, and of lectures, are always impossible to quantify. Both these advantages were available for a small subscription from 1834.

Where education is concerned, the most significant period in the history of the Institutes was the 50 or so years before the establishment of the Technical Institute in Park Street in 1910. Since the 1850s the Institutes had been responding to Henry Cole's initiatives, and in 1857 art classes under C. C. Pyne began. Science classes were started by the Working Men's Institute in the mid-seventies. Under the Technical Instruction Acts of 1889 and 1891 local authorities could give grants for technical instruction. The Institute received such a grant from 1890 for the classes run by Captain Campbell.

A free ticket to the 1878 Paris Exhibition competed for by students in the art classes was won by Miss S. M. Baker of Gomshall Station. Other working men students went to the 1889 Exhibition and wrote reports on it.

After education became compulsory in 1870, Guildford schools followed the same patterns of change as schools elsewhere. A School Board was set up in 1883. Guildford had its own Education Committee responsible for primary education from 1902-44. The County's provision for secondary schooling included the building of the first non-private secondary school for girls in the town in the Farnham Road in the years immediately preceding the First World War.

Since the University of Surrey settled in the shadow of the Cathedral, and took the Institute under its wing, educational impetus has carried the town onwards into paths sometimes new, albeit still virtuous and noble.

121. The only known representation of the building in front of Holy Trinity Church founded by Thomas Baker in 1579 to house a market for rye, the rents of which were to support a schoolmaster to teach up to 30 'poore mennes sonnes ... to wright and reade Englishe and to cast accompts expertly'. This 19th-century drawing by C. C. Pyne must be a copy of some unknown original, since the building was demolished in 1758.

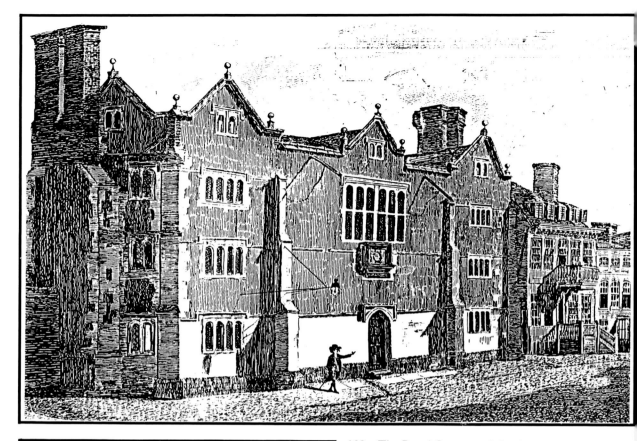

122. The Royal Grammar School, engraved from a watercolour by the Reverend Thomas Russell, Rector of West Clandon, c.1778. John Austen began the master's house, the right wing (1569), and George Austen completed it (1586); William Hammond began the Usher's House, the left wing (completed 1582) and gallery across the front (1571); the schoolhouse across the back of the courtyard was begun in 1557. The schoolmaster Samuel Cole (1769-1804) is said to be the figure standing outside.

123. Notice by the Mayor Henry Flutter, 1765, on the same day as he had called a public meeting. The Grammar School was managed by the Corporation, and at a Guild Merchant on 14 February it was resolved to suspend payment of the salary of the Master, the Reverend John Pearsall, because of his 'intolerable negligence and misbehaviour', including wrongfully charging fees, so that there had been no pupils in the school for a year. It took some time and expense to put matters right.

124.   Advertisements for some Guildford girls' schools of the 18th and 19th centuries. The whereabouts of Mrs. Chardin's boarding school is not known, but in 1779 the daughter of the miller in Abinger was a pupil at Mrs. Frances Yalden's school. Madame Delay's School on the Mount and Mrs. Bayston's at no. 54 Quarry Street were short-lived examples of a familiar type.

125. Tower of Archbishop Abbott School, 1856-1933, and the *Crown*. Created to utilise the site of the Manufacture, and using its funds and those of Baker's School, this establishment, a 'Middle Class School' to educate boys unsuited for a grammar school education in 'modern' and practical subjects, had an excellent reputation but was eventually forced to close due to lack of funds.

126. Archbishop Abbott School boys in the school yard, with the hospital behind them. Of these 62 boys aged seven to 14, free places were awarded to 30 'Baker's Boys', and there should have been an equal number of fee-payers. There are apparently two masters and two monitors at the time this photograph was taken, early this century.

127. Charlotteville Board School was opened in 1886, and enlarged in 1890 to accommodate nearly one thousand pupils in three divisions: Infants, Boys and Girls. In 1928 it became Guildford (Selective) Central School, and in 1945 Pewley County Secondary School. It extends down a steep hill, and is now an adult education centre.

128. Pupils of Charlotteville School with the Watkin Shield for needlework in 1927. Left to right, from the back: A. Hines, V. Airey, M. Oxborrow, E. Hollingshead and E. Chitty; Mr. J. Gardiner (headmaster), V. Sheppard, M. Cooper, H. Stickley, M. Farley, I. Mitchell, H. Whitbourn, and Miss Gaines; E. Hill, L. Knowles, C. Balchin, E. Edwards, A. Coles, O. Balchin and E. Cuthbert. The examiners stated that the work submitted was the best in the history of the competition.

129. John Springfield, cobbler, of Chertsey Street. A Methodist, he was one of the volunteers who helped in Mr. Robert Macdonald's Evening Mission School, where he taught his own craft. According to the romantic story of his life as related by his granddaughter Zillah, he was the son of Jumbaloowagee, a Zanzibar chief, escaped from slavery, and was given his name by the captain of the *Victoria* on which he served from 1864 to 1867. He married an English girl and their daughter Miriam attended Miss Bloxham's school in Guildford. John died in 1891.

130. The Mayor, James Baker, with the Mayoress, and ex-Mayor Colonel Lane, at Stoke Schools in January 1908. He presented a Union Jack to the school in recognition of the children's help at a recent naval concert. The children were given cards on which was a Union Jack; the Mayor reminded them that the Empire was one big family, and Colonel Lane that the flag stood for duty and discipline.

131.   Captain C. D. Campbell, Her Majesty's Indian Navy, 1813-1904. From 1869-89 he was Honorary Secretary of the Guildford Science and Art Classes, which were attended by working men and young people. He also gave lectures on such subjects as the scientific aspects of the temperance question and travels. He was a pioneer in the use of the tricycle, constructing one to his own design in the 1860s.

132.   Poster announcing the drawing class run by the Working Men's Institute, 1866-67, and listing the prizes given by patrons, who include the artist and teacher C. C. Pyne. Some prizes are given for 'art' (a sketch of a cottage at St Catherine's), but most for geometrical and architectural drawings.

Guildford Working Men's Institution.

SEASON 1866-67.

DRAWING CLASS.

President—J. R. CAPRON, ESQ.

Patrons—

THE LORD CHIEF JUSTICE BOVILL.
C. C. PYNE, ESQ.
THE REV. R. B. MATTHEWS.
T. J. SELLS, ESQ.
MR. THOS. GILL.

MR. W. H. HALL.
E. MARR, ESQ.
MR. J. HEATHER.
W. W. POCOCK, ESQ.
R. GARTH, ESQ., M.P.

LIST OF PRIZES.

1 and 2. THE LORD CHIEF JUSTICE BOVILL has given 10s. for familiar objects, in two prizes, 6s. for the best in second grade, and 4s. for the best in first grade, to be competed for on Thursday Evening, May 23rd.

3, 4, and 5.' And likewise 10s. to be expended on prizes for the pupils in first grade; these prizes to be competed for on the following Evenings, viz :—Freehand, May 2nd.; Model, May 9th.; Geometry, May 16th.

6. C. C. PYNE, ESQ. has offered a prize, value 10s., for the best six sheets of problems in perspective, from "Burchett's Linear Perspective," viz :—plate 5, figure 22; plate 6, figure 23; plate 12, figure 33; plate 13, figure 34; plate 17, figure 38; and plate 18, figure 39; size of each sheet, 14 in. × 9 in. to be neatly executed in ink; the working lines may be left in pencil.

133. Guildford High School for Girls, founded in 1888. In 1887 Miss Morton took over, at the Reverend Francis Paynter's request, his parish hall in Haydon Place from Mrs. Beeney's Guildford College and established a High School there. It was soon taken on by the Church Schools Company. Its earliest pupils included daughters of many of the town's principal families: Alice and Margaret Jacobs, Ethel Moon and Lilian Carling, as well as Julia and Evelyn Paynter.

134. The County School for Girls, opened July 1914. This, the first state secondary school for girls in Guildford, originated in a pupil-teacher training school started in 1904 by Miss Morton, the headmistress of the High School. The buildings in the Farnham Road were opened by Dr. T. E. Page of Charterhouse who said 'this school is exactly the type which does most good'. In August the buildings were taken over for use as an annexe of the Royal Surrey County Hospital opposite.

135. The Congregational Sunday School marching to Shalford Park, probably in the 1890s. This very popular
Sunday School drew children from other denominations. It occupied the Black Horse Lane Chapel from 1868 until
1884 when new schools were built behind the North Street Church. In 1851 there were 136 scholars attending in the
morning and 122 in the afternoon. This is presumably their outing.

136.   Opening of the Technical Institute in Park Street, by Mrs. G. F. Watts, 16 March 1910. Among those present were the Chairman of Surrey Education Committee, the Mayor and other County and Borough dignitaries. Mrs. Watts spoke of the beauty and appropriateness of the building, honouring both science and art. Paid for jointly by County and Borough Councils, there were classrooms, laboratories and workshops for up to 700 pupils.

Recreation, Association, Dissipation

In the 16th century the court books record punishments imposed on adults who played cards when they should have been in church. The Grammar School boys played cricket and watched bear-baiting. In the 18th century the bowling green moved from the further side of North Street to its present position above the castle. The existence of a cock-pit shows that there was cock-fighting. No doubt many citizens found their way to Merrow Downs during the races, which began early in the 18th century.

In 1619 the Hallwardens paid six shillings 'to players not to play here'. Perhaps a play was sometimes performed just outside the borough boundary: towards the end of the 18th century Mr. Smallpeice was paying rent for a barn in the manor of Stoke 'where the play was lately'. In 1788 Henry Thornton built and opened a theatre in the old Red Lion Yard, running alongside the new street. It was probably not unlike the Georgian Theatre in Richmond. Thornton put on plays there for some years, and was followed by his son-in-law Edward Barnett, who embellished the building with a new curtain drop, act drops and 'a variety of new Scenery'. His performances were patronised by many of the local gentry. Every season between 1834 and 1838 the benefit for Miss Gordon, of the Theatre Royal, Drury Lane, was sponsored by Joseph Hockley the Town Clerk. He died in 1838 aged 52 and she did not play again in Guildford.

The 19th century saw an ever increasing range of indoor and outdoor entertainments, activities and clubs. Productions by local groups, including the very active dramatic group of the 13th Surrey Rifle Volunteers, and other companies of actors and musicians, were interspersed among those by visiting professional troupes.

One theatre closed; another opened. Several cinemas were opened during the 20th century and, thanks to Claud Powell, a Guildford orchestra and operatic society came into existence.

137. 'Concise Memoirs of two Celebrated Fighting Cocks.' 'Birchin Yellow [*far right*] ... fought ll battles, after which he was made a brood cock. Thirty-six of his sons fought at the Royal Pit, Westminster, on one main, 32 of which won. Ginger Wing Red [*right*] fought at Westminster and won ... after which he won the two following years at Guildford.'

BY DESIRE, AND UNDER THE PATRONAGE
OF THE RIGHT HONORABLE

Lord Grantley,
Steward of the Races.

THEATRE GUILDFORD

On WEDNESDAY Evening, JULY 11th. 1832,

Will be presented SHERIDAN's celebrated Comedy of

The Rivals.

Falkland........Mr. BARRY.	Captain Absolute.......Mr. CATHCART.
Sir Anthony Absolute........Mr. BARNETT.	Acres......Mr. WYATT. David....Mr. RENAUD.

Sir Lucius O'Trigger............Mr. GRIFFITH.

Fag........Mr. PITT.	Coachman......Mr. YARNOLD.	Boy......Mr. CLAYTON.
Lydia Languish......Mrs. BARNETT.		Lucy......Mrs. GRIFFITH.
Mrs. Malaprop..............Mrs. RENAUD.		Julia Melville..............Mrs. FAWCETT.

END OF THE PLAY,

A favorite Song, by Miss SOMERVILLE.

A COMIC SONG, BY MR. RENAUD.

A SAILOR's HORNPIPE, by Mr. PITT.

A Comic Song, by Mr. WYATT.

A Scotch Dance, by Master ELLIOT.

The whole to conclude with the highly popular Comic Drama, called

Deaf as a Post.

Captain Templeton......Mr. CATHCART.	Old Walton......Mr. RENAUD.
Crupper....Mr. YARNOLD. Gallop....Mr. PAICE.	Tristram Sappy....Mr. BARNETT.
Mrs. Plumpley............Mrs. RENAUD.	Sophy..........Mrs. GRIFFITH.
Amy......Miss FRY.	Sally Maggs......Mrs. BARNETT.

Doors to be opened at SEVEN, and to commence at Half-past. Second Price at Nine.

BOXES 3s.   PIT 2s.   GALLERY 1s.

☞ TICKETS may be had of Mr. BARNETT, at Mr. Fuller's, Spital Street, and at
THE LIBRARY, where Places for the Boxes may be taken.

[Russells, Printers.]

138.   Poster for a performance of *The Rivals* by R. B. Sheridan in Guildford Theatre, 11 July 1832.
Lord Grantley sponsored this performance by Edward Barnett's company, of a play written by his
sister-in-law's grandfather. Cathcart was the star of the company. This season the newcomers
included Mr. Griffith from Bath, Mr. Pitt from Oxford and Mr. Yarnold from Newbury.

139. St Catherine's Fair, by Miss Swaine, c.1900. Richard de Wauncey, rector of St Nicholas, built the chapel in the early 1300s. In 1308 he obtained a licence to hold an annual fair around the feast of St Matthew the Evangelist. The fair continued after the chapel fell into disuse in the 16th century, being held on 2 October from 1752, but ceased before 1914. In 1835 and 1837 William Swayne of Merrow was paid for carting a booth to St Catherine's Fair.

140. 'An attempt to put down St Catherine's Hill Fair, October 1832.' Cholera struck a number of times in Guildford during the early 19th century, largely because of inadequate drainage, and wells next to cess pits. The last epidemic in Guildford was in 1866. This was not the only Guildford fair the nervous – or spoilsports – tried to stop.

Catherine Hill Fair.

Cholera Morbus!

Between twenty and thirty thousand of our fellow Countrymen have died suddenly of Cholera Morbus, within the last few months.

Experience has proved that Intoxication provokes Cholera, and that large Assemblages of People, such as Catherine Hill Fair, provoke Intoxication.

Such an Assemblage on Brandon Hill near Bristol, was severely visited. Other similar incidents might be cited. Some Fairs have been altogether put off for this year. Guildford and its vicinity have been hitherto spared in much mercy.

The Devil has been as busy as usual in diverse places with Gin and Beer; and ALMIGHTY GOD, in just judgment, has sent a Pestilence to help the Devil in consigning multitudes to an unprepared Eternity.

Who then will provoke GOD? Who will go to Catherine Hill Fair, and meet thousands of idle, and hundreds of drunken people from the surrounding Country?

Granting that you have no regard for your own life, which however is not the case, though some of you may think it a fine manly thing to say so; have you no regard for your Father, Mother, Husband, Wife, Children? And will you for the sake of a paltry idle gratification of a few hours, run the risk of having a Cholera Corpse brought home to the bosom of your family? Or will you venture to incur the anguish of recovering yourself, after having been the guilty instrument of communicating Disease and Death to others?

No, I won't. Then don't go to Catherine Hill Fair!!!

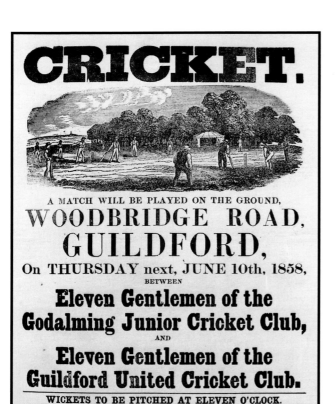

CRICKET.

A MATCH WILL BE PLAYED ON THE GROUND,

WOODBRIDGE ROAD,
GUILDFORD,

On THURSDAY next, JUNE 10th, 1858,

BETWEEN

Eleven Gentlemen of the
Godalming Junior Cricket Club,

AND

Eleven Gentlemen of the
Guildford United Cricket Club.

WICKETS TO BE PITCHED AT ELEVEN O'CLOCK.

Dinner provided at the "Prince of Wales," at Two o'Clock.

ANDREWS, PRINTER, GUILDFORD.

141. Notice of a cricket match in 1858. The club playing in this match was not the present Guildford club, which was founded in 1883. On this ground in the Woodbridge Road, used for drilling and many other activities as well as cricket, the new Cattle Market was built in 1894. The present ground was given by Sir Harry Waechter in 1911.

142. Fair in North Street on the day of the Cattle Market, held there between 1865 and 1890. The fair is in the open space east of the *Horse and Groom* where the Grammar School boys once played their games. The *Crown* almost blocks the street this side of Pimms. The *Horse and Groom* is selling Crooke's beer from the brewery just across the Town Bridge.

LARGE HALL, COUNTY & BOROUGH HALLS, GUILDFORD,
TWO NIGHTS ONLY—THURSDAY and FRIDAY, 13th and 14th SEPTEMBER.
Tickets to be obtained of Messrs. STENT & SONS, Booksellers, 32 High Street.

NOT GREAT, NOR GREATER, BUT THE GREATEST !

FEMALE CHRISTYS

Minstrel Organization in the World

TWELVE SYMMETRICAL FEMALE FORMS.

A BEVY OF BEAUTY,	THE OCTOROON,
THE BLONDE,	THE QUADROON,
THE BRUNETTE,	THE MULATTO,

AND THE

BEAUTIFUL CREOLES

An Earthquake opening up a Volcano, from which gushes forth a living stream of Mirth.
The Pinnacle of Artistic and Unalloyed Refinement reached at last.

THE NAME OF ANDY MERRILEES'

ARMOUR + CLAD + AMAZON + FEMALE + CHRISTYS

Is a Household Word all over the Land.

These Popular Lady Artistes have, by arduous efforts, won for themselves a reputation
which at once places them at the head, and the public treasure up their names as
the Sweetest Buds in Memory's Golden Casket.

MIRTH, MUSIC, MIMICRY, AND COMEDY.

Patronized by the very Best of Society !
Perfectly Free from all Objectionable Features !
Particularly Adapted to Suit all Classes !

A Grand Consolidation of brightest Stars in the Amusement Firmament, presenting a Programme of Unsurpassed Elegance, an
Entertainment in which every feature is offered in a manner which makes a Successful Imitation an utter Impossibility.

THE LARGEST, MOST COMPLETE, AND EFFECTIVE COMBINATION OF

LADY SOLO INSTRUMENTALISTS

With any Minstrel Organization in the British Isles, surpassing all previous efforts—the
happy blending of Harmony with Humour, the ideal of Pathos, and Cream of Mirth.

Hilarity precipitated indiscriminately at Eight p.m. Doors open Half-an-hour previously.
ADMISSION—FRONT SEATS, 2s; SECOND SEATS, 1s; BACK SEATS, 6d.
Sole Proprietor, - Mr. ANDY MERRILEES. Business Manager, - Mr. HARRY BATTERSBY.

BEAUTIFUL SCENES, NEW AND ELEGANT !

143. Poster for an entertainment in the County and Borough Halls, *c.*1890.

BOROUGH HALL,
GUILDFORD.

Saturday, August 22nd, 1891; Afternoon at 3, Evening at 8.

Mr. CLARENCE SOUNES (Lessee and Manager, New Theatre Royal, Aldershot) has the pleasure to announce the appearance of

THE

AFRICAN NATIVE CHOIR

Under the Direction Mr. N. VERT.

THE ONLY KAFFIR CHOIR OF ITS KIND IN THE WORLD.

Representing Seven distinct Tribes, viz :

AMAXOSA, FINGO, TEMBU, BAPEDI, BASUTO, ZULU, and CAPE.

Soprani.
E. XINIWE.
MALABESE MANYE.
J. JONKERS.

Contralti.
MAKHOMO MANYE.
MBIKAZI NOBENGULA.
F. GQOBA.
A. JONAS.

S. KOOPMAN.
J. XINIWE.

Tenori.
NELI MABANDLA.
G. McLELLAN.
J. MBONGWE.

Bassi.
P. XINIWE.
J. SEMOUSE.
S. KONONGO.
W. MAJIZA.

Manager of Choir, - WALTER E. LETTY.
Musical Director and Secretary, - - J. H. BALMER, R.A.M.
Accompanist, - - Miss CLARK.

WHO WILL GIVE

TWO GRAND CONCERTS

ON

SATURDAY AFTERNOON AND EVENING, AUGUST 22nd 1891,

Doors open, Afternoon, at **2.30.** *Commene at* **3** *o'clock. Carriages at* **4.45.**

Doors open, Evening, at **7.30.** *Commence at* **8.** *Carriages at* **9.45.**

OBJECT OF VISIT.

The aim and object of the Visit of this Choir to England is to interest the Public in the Internal Social, and Material Progress of South Africa and its Native Population, by the establishment of Trade and Technical Schools, for teaching Manual Handicrafts, Domestic Economy, Cookery, Nursing, and such other Useful Arts as are essential to the future well-being of the Native People of Africa.

Prices : — Reserved and Numbered Seats, 3s. Second Seats, 2s.
Admission, - One Shilling.
Plan of Hall, Tickets, and Programmes at the usual Agents, or by Letter or Telegram to
Mr. SOUNES, Theatre, Aldershot.

P. T. O.

144. Concert by a Native Choir from South Africa, 22 August 1891. Part of the object of this concert was to raise money in order to be able to teach the Africans practical handicrafts and other skills. The performance included a mixture of African music (e.g. *Mgwelo engena tentyi,* a 'Wayside Kaffir Song') and English songs.

145: 'The Old Cycle Shop' in Quarry Street at the
end of the 19th century. Cycling was a popular
pastime, as well as a way of getting about.
Guildford Cycling Club was established in 1885;
there were also clubs in individual firms, and based
in inns. This building was the *Good Intent* public
house and later the Good Intent Apartment House
for Men. Demolished in the 1960s, it has been
replaced by flats.

146. The short-lived rink in Woodbridge Road
was used for both ice and roller skating. It was
visited in 1887 by Russian skaters. Another skating
rink in Farnham Road was proposed.

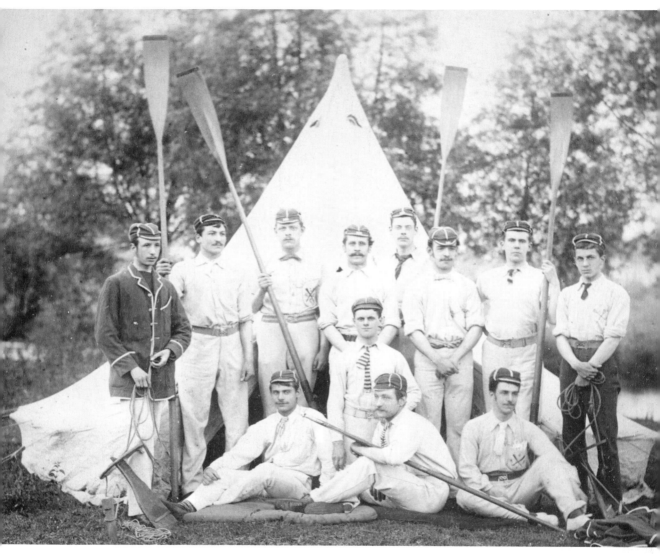

147.   Guildford Amateur Rowing Club, 1885. The Rowing Club is the oldest of the existing sporting organisations in the town, founded in 1883. Their boat-house is still close to the *Jolly Farmer*. Left to right, standing: W. J. Bone, S. Bird, W. A. Harris, H. S. Folker, W. R. Harris, J. Bakewell, P. H. Lacon, H. V. Lunn; kneeling: G. Gwinn; sitting: G. Harrison, W. Maynard, Jordan.

148. The Theatre Royal in the County and Borough Halls, 1912. Converted from the larger hall, this theatre opened on 9 December with a musical *The Girl in the Train*. Guildford had had no theatre since that in Market Street became a warehouse in 1864. This theatre could seat 1,050. The auditorium was decorated in white and gold, and the transformation was enthusiastically received. The last performance before Surrey County Council closed it for structural alterations in 1932 was the Cockyolly Company's *Alice* for the Lewis Carroll centenary.

149. The cinema in Woodbridge Road was the second to open in Guildford, in the barn which can be seen through the gateway. This photograph was taken just before it was rebuilt in 1923, on this site, as indicated by the arrows. The 1923 building still exists.

150. The Guildford Symphony Orchestra, 28 November 1923, with their Leader, S. F. Blagrove. Claud Powell started this orchestra in 1919, in which year he also founded the County School of Music. He conducted the Guildford Choral Society and was involved with Guildford Repertory Theatre. It was he who persuaded Graham Robertson to write the pageant *The Town of the Ford* (1925) and he put on A. P. Herbert and Thomas Dunhill's comic opera *Tantivy Towers*. He was the key figure in Guildford music for 40 years, dying in 1959. This was the last of the eight concerts in 1923. Roger Quilter and J. B. McEwen joined Claud Powell to conduct their own works.

Wider Still and Wider

The boundaries of the borough were enlarged in 1835 to coincide with those of the 1832 parliamentary constituency. This included those areas of Stoke which had for some time been part of Guildford in all but name. Apart from two small further parts of Stoke, one containing the Union Workhouse (1888), the next addition was that of 1904. Merrow successfully resisted inclusion at this date, becoming part of the borough in 1933, together with a large area extending mostly northwards. Guildford Park and Onslow Village had been included in 1922. There was one further addition, in 1954, before 1974 saw the union of the old borough with Guildford Rural District Council in the new Guildford Borough Council.

These increases in area and population were accompanied by the building of large new council and other estates, with concomitant facilities in the way of churches and schools, as well as the ordinary amenities of civilised living. The museum and the hospitals were enlarged, Onslow Village was created and Stoke Park was bought. Guildford became a separate diocese in 1927, and in 1936 the building of the cathedral on Stag Hill began. Expansion of all kinds continued up to the outbreak of war in 1939.

151. St Saviour's Church, Woodbridge Road. This church, built in 1899 to replace an iron church, was the closest to the centre of Guildford of all the churches built within his parish by the Reverend Francis Paynter of Stoke. Mrs. Paynter laid the foundation stone.

The Surrey Advertiser was Founded 2nd April 1864 by Joseph Whittaker Barfoot and Published by him at 10 High Street Guildford

The Surrey Advertiser first appeared as a Monthly Advertising Medium, next as a Fortnightly Publication, ultimately becoming a Weekly Newspaper on the 30th July 1864

No. 1. April 1864. Printed by William Stent 32 High Street Guildford
No. 2. May 7. 1864 1/2 Printed by Joseph Billing Railway Esplanade Guildford
No. 67 Sep. 30 1865
No. 68 Oct. 7 1865 1/2 Printed by the Proprietor Joseph Whittaker Barfoot at 10 High Street Guildford
No. 170 Nov. 16 1867

152. Advertisement for the first issue of *The Surrey Advertiser* in 1864, with details of subsequent history written on the mount. This was the first newspaper to be printed in Guildford, and one of the first in Surrey.

153. The new diocese of Guildford, carved out of the diocese of Winchester and almost co-extensive with the ancient archdeaconry of Surrey, came into being in 1927. There was as yet no cathedral, and Holy Trinity Church was the pro-cathedral. The cathedral was not consecrated until 17 May 1961 by the Archbishop of Canterbury. Here the Lord Lieutenant and Sheriff wait in the courtyard of Abbot's Hospital to enter Holy Trinity Church for the enthronement of the first Bishop, 12 July 1927.

154. Ram Corner decorated to celebrate the coronation of Edward VII and Queen Alexandra, 1902. With an archway erected in the narrow section of the street (13 ft. 6 ins. wide until widened by the removal of the *Ram* in 1913) it is easy to visualise this as the old eastern entrance to the town.

155. The President of the Local Government Board, D. Addison, M.P., cutting the first sod in connection with the Stoughton Housing Scheme, 12 June 1919. In November 1918 the Council resolved to build 300 houses. The first 85 were to be built on eight acres at Stoughton: four with four bedrooms and parlour, 50 with three bedrooms and parlour and 31 with three bedrooms and no parlour. They were designed by E. L. Lunn. More than 300 applications were received for the first houses completed.

156. Plan by Messrs. Hodgson Lunn & Co. for the Guildown Estate, 1926. General Longbourne of Loseley, the developer, has constructed a road with 12 one-acre plots fronting it. Houses to be built must be worth at least £2,000. The area where the pagan Anglo-Saxon burials were found is hatched in plot no. 4.

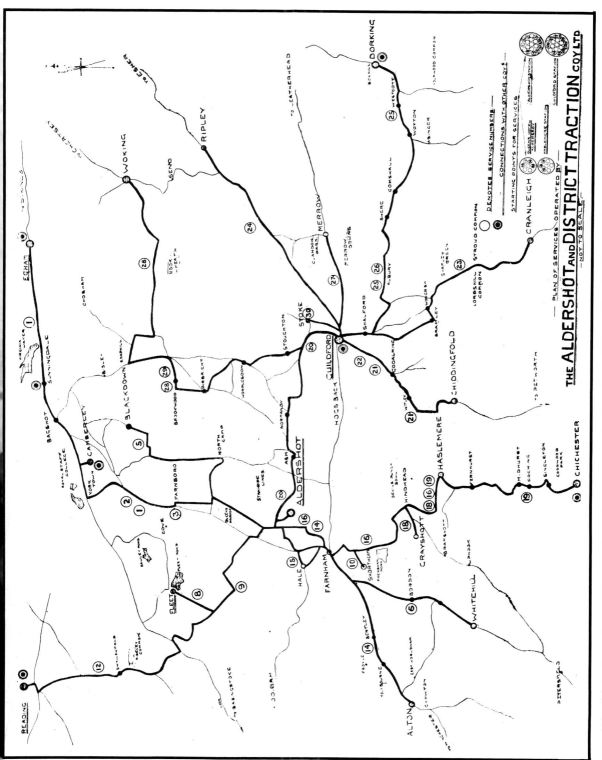

157. 'Motor Buses Galore.' This map shows the buses run by the Aldershot and District Traction Company in August 1921. The company was particularly pleased with the long runs, to Reading, Egham, Alton and Chichester, where connections to other places could be established.

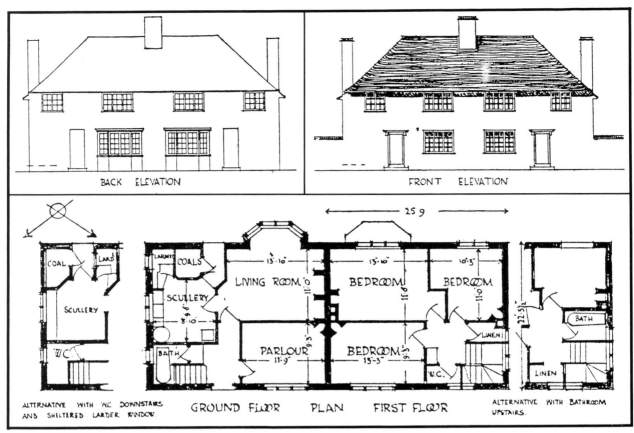

BACK ELEVATION

FRONT ELEVATION

ALTERNATIVE WITH WC DOWNSTAIRS AND SHELTERED LARDER WINDOW

GROUND FLOOR PLAN FIRST FLOOR

ALTERNATIVE WITH BATHROOM UPSTAIRS.

COAL LARD

SCULLERY

W.C.

LARDER COALS

SCULLERY

BATH

LIVING ROOM

PARLOUR

BEDROOM

BEDROOM

BEDROOM

LINEN

W.C.

BATH

LINEN

25 9

158. Onslow Village prospectus, 1920. One of the types of house to be built on the estate. It was F. F. Smallpeice's idea to build a Garden City in Guildford. Lord Onslow discussed the matter with Mr. Litchfield, and decided on which land, and Guildford Corporation and the Ministry of Health backed the scheme. A Public Utility Company was formed. The project was a success.

159. Stoke Park in the early part of this century. Stoke Park, probably built by William Aldersey shortly before 1800, was inherited from his successor Nathaniel Hillier by the 4th Earl of Onslow, who sold it in 1879 to James Budgett. In 1925 Budgett sold the house and park and Burchatt's Farm to the Corporation. As soon as the occupier's lease ran out it was leased to the County Council for a Technical College.

Fighting Men and Working Women

In the days when there was a beacon on Guildown to warn of an enemy landing, and when every man was obliged to turn out to practise at the butts with his bow, all males between the ages of 15 and 60 were potential soldiers. When there was no longer a danger of invasion, however, regular drilling ceased. It was revived in 1757 with a Militia Bill, which introduced a not dissimilar system of obligation. With the outbreak of the Napoleonic Wars, the Surrey Militia was embodied. Barracks were built on the Friary estate in 1794 to house regular troops in transit. The Militia was revived once more in 1852 and a new Militia Depot, designed by Lord Lovelace, was created at the bottom of North Street in 1854. This became redundant when Stoughton Barracks were built in 1876 for the Queen's Regiment, to which the 2nd Royal Surrey Militia was attached. The Volunteer Rifles were formed in 1859, the predecessors of the territorials. Guildford men volunteered readily to fight when there was need. Many went to the Boer War, and the Surrey Militia received a warm welcome home on their return. During the First World War Guildford claimed its high recruitment figures were a record.

Women of all classes did their bit, working in factories and in many other jobs, including on the land. 'Women of the more educated class' were found to be 'as a rule more accustomed to the management of horses'.

160. The Friary House in the early 19th century. Built by John Murray, Earl of Annandale, in about 1610 on the site of the Dominican Friary, both Charles I and Charles II stayed in the house, later used for public events and as a school. It was bought for barracks in 1794, and used as officers' quarters until pulled down in 1818.

161. (*Above*) The Parade Ground in the Militia Depôt in the 1860s. The 2nd Royal Surrey Militia used the depot as a centre for their three weeks' annual training until 1876, when the buildings were sold for civilian use.

162. (*Facing page, below*) Guildford Volunteers in camp, August 1888. The 13th Surrey Rifle Volunteers had become a Volunteer Battalion of the Queen's Regiment in 1883. This camp is at Denbies, Dorking. Private W. R. Harris, left in the back row, became the Registrar of Births and Deaths in Guildford.

163. (*Right*) A newspaper boy gives the news of the Relief of Mafeking, 19 May 1900. The nation had waited with bated breath for Colonel R. S. Baden-Powell's despatches from the beleaguered town. When he returned to England the boys of his old school, Charterhouse, fêted him and Guildford presented him with the Freedom of the Borough in June 1903. In 1908 he founded the Boy Scout movement.

164. The old Union Workhouse in use as a Military Hospital during the First World War. Built in Stoke parish in 1838, with an infirmary wing added in 1896, it was increasingly used only as a hospital for the sick poor, though, apart from its period as a military hospital, remaining under the Guardians till 1930. Then managed by Surrey County Council, it began to develop as a general hospital. The pedimented arch was the original Workhouse entrance.

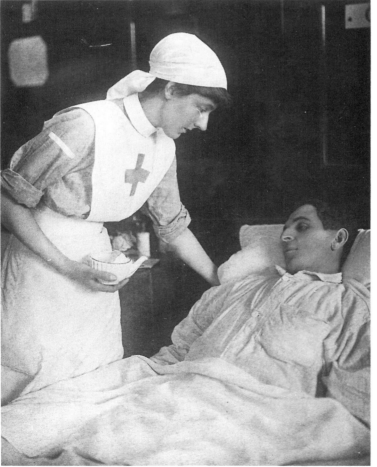

165. A Red Cross nurse, Miss Lunn, and a patient in the Red Cross annexe. This is probably not the County School for Girls, used as an annexe to the Royal Surrey County Hospital during the First World War, but Clandon Park Red Cross Hospital, run by Lady Onslow from 1914-19.

166. & 167. During the First World War women took over many essential jobs to release men for the front. This rural postwoman, Miss Bullinger, is wearing a divided skirt. The landgirl is Miss Cledgey. Women were slow to volunteer for work on the land, though by the end of 1916 there were known to be 1,469 in Surrey. It must have been exceptional for a girl to plough with a horse. Shortage of labour encouraged mechanisation, but even at the end of the war there were only 79 'government tractors' in use on Surrey farms.

1942 Pep talk from a V.I.P.

168. Pep-talk from a V.I.P., at Dennis Bros. Woodbridge Works, 1942. Before and during the First World War Dennis were building the 'subvention vehicle'. Before the war a subsidy of £110 was paid to the owner of a subvention lorry, from whom it would then be purchased in the event of war. In the Second World War they went over entirely to war production, building among other vehicles the Churchill tank. The work force comprised both sexes.

Big Business and the Factory Floor

Between 1890 and 1914 the country-town workshops such as Filmer & Mason and Jacobs were replaced by three large industrial undertakings, all to become known world-wide. Billing's the printers did not start in Guildford, as did the other two, but came from Woking to Railway Esplanade at the station end of Walnut Tree Close. They developed and expanded into one of the most versatile printers in the country, claiming that they could print in any (written) language. They also printed music. In 1924 the work-force was among the largest in the town, and was always treated with exceptional consideration.

Dennis Brothers started by making bicycles, with a shop at the bottom of the High Street. They quickly moved into motor vehicles, devising improvements as they went. A 1902 catalogue of 'The Oldest Motor Makers in England' stresses 'scientific design and accurate workmanship' and lists cars and a converted quadricycle. Expansion was so fast that they moved from a works in the old barracks to a purpose-built factory on the corner of Onslow Street and Bridge Street, and then to the Woodbridge Hill site between 1900 and 1905. No cars were made after 1913. The firm specialised in buses, vans and lorries, fire engines, and several types of vehicle for municipal use. All these were sold throughout the world, the most prosperous years for the company being 1946-51. Taken over in 1972, and subject to re-organisation in 1985, little of the original nature or products of the company remains.

The third firm also started in a small way, indeed even by chance. Arthur Drummond was a painter who enjoyed making models and could not find a convenient small lathe. Having devised one for himself he had so many requests that soon after 1900 he went into production. The firm developed, on a site at Ryde's Hill north-west of Guildford, and in 1962 employed 300 men. Drummond lathes turned all the crank-shafts and propellor shafts for Bristol engines during the Second World War. The factory closed in 1980.

All these firms trained many apprentices in specialised skills and all recruited workers from outside the town, and secured great loyalty and pride in the firm among their workers. Could this go some way to explain the nature of the Labour movement in Guildford? The Trades and Labour Council, a body drawn, as its name implies, from all trades and industries in Guildford, was in existence by 1913. Their minutes record attempts to prevent the exploitation of workers, such as protests against the low wages paid by local firms making manhole covers, and earned by women working on the roads in Merrow. In June 1920 they expressed opposition to the involvement of members in encouraging militaristic attitudes in Boy Scouts and Girl Guides. They met frequently during the General Strike, and prepared the *Guildford Strike Bulletin*. This Council continues to be an active body, keeping a watchful eye on all Labour matters.

169. Billing's letterhead in the 1890s, showing the works opposite the station. Joseph Billing, a devout Baptist, ran his successful business on Christian principles. The firm's skills in foreign language printing were used for bibles and missionary literature. They also printed scientific and technical periodicals and books.

BILLING AND SONS.
Book, Magazine, and General Printers.

STEREOTYPING AND ELECTROTYPING.

NOT RESPONSIBLE FOR PROPERTY DESTROYED BY FIRE.

December 10 1891

170. Billing's works in Walnut Tree Close from the air, *c.*1960. Between 1926 and 1962 the entire works moved northwards along the river. The new buildings were more convenient for the larger machines in use, and for parking lorries.

171. Boys at Charterhouse School working at metal turning in 1909 – an early example of technological education. These lathes almost certainly came from Drummond's factory at Rydes Hill. Started by Arthur Drummond as a hobby, to provide a small lathe for model engineering, the business expanded and enjoyed a high reputation for its multi-tool and copying lathes, and gear-cutting machines.

172. The Dennis Factory at Woodbridge in 1926: 'the View Room'. Women are working alongside the men in one of the huge workshops, making parts for the increasing range of vehicles then being manufactured. Most vehicle production ceased at Woodbridge in 1985, and the remaining work on the site will cease shortly.

173. Dennis Brothers' pride in their product: an advertising van in 1929. The 30-cwt. van was a very popular line. Like every vehicle manufactured at Woodbridge, only the chassis was standard; bodywork was made according to each customer's wishes.

GENERAL ELECTION, 1918.

Polling Day—December 14th, 1918.

To the Electors of the Guildford Division.

63a, North Street,
Guildford,
December 4th, 1918.

WILLIAM BENNETT,
LABOUR CANDIDATE.

LADIES AND GENTLEMEN,

As I have been unanimously selected by the organised workers and members affiliated to the Labour Party in this division as their Parliamentary Candidate, I respectfully solicit the favour of your vote and interest at the forthcoming Election.

In so supporting me, you will be voting for the measures of reform outlined in the attached programme, rather than for myself.

In my opinion, these alterations are long overdue : we cannot go back to the old conditions of penury and starvation, which were all that society used to allow to millions of workers; and if we are to have a systematic and orderly reconstruction of society, it can only be done by the workers themselves, through their delegates elected in a constitutional manner by the vote.

The time has gone by for trusting to the promises of politicians, over whom the people have no hold once they have received a blank cheque for five years of power.

The Labour Party Programme has come from the people themselves; every item has been discussed and passed by the delegates of millions of organised workers, hand and brain, and it is the lowest minimum of justice we are prepared to accept.

174. Part of the election manifesto of the first Labour candidate to stand in a Guildford election, William Bennett, 14 December 1918. Born at Oakhill in Somerset 45 years earlier, he had been a chemist at Newton Abbot where he was active in the formation of a Labour Party. He resigned as manager of Timothy White's in Guildford to give all his time to this election. His sympathies, he said, were 'wholly with the toilers and moilers'; 'Labour only can liberate the workers … and make life worth living for them'. The result was announced on 28 December – Horne 13,149, Bennett 5,078.

175. 'Twilight in Guildford' by William Hyde White, c.1906. In a wet winter dusk, between Trinity Hospital and Trinity Church, a cab waits and a paper-boy stands hopefully. Below the pinnacles of Sainsbury's are the bright lights of the County Club. The sudden plunge of the wide street beyond is still, as it has been for many centuries, what everyone remembers about Guildford.

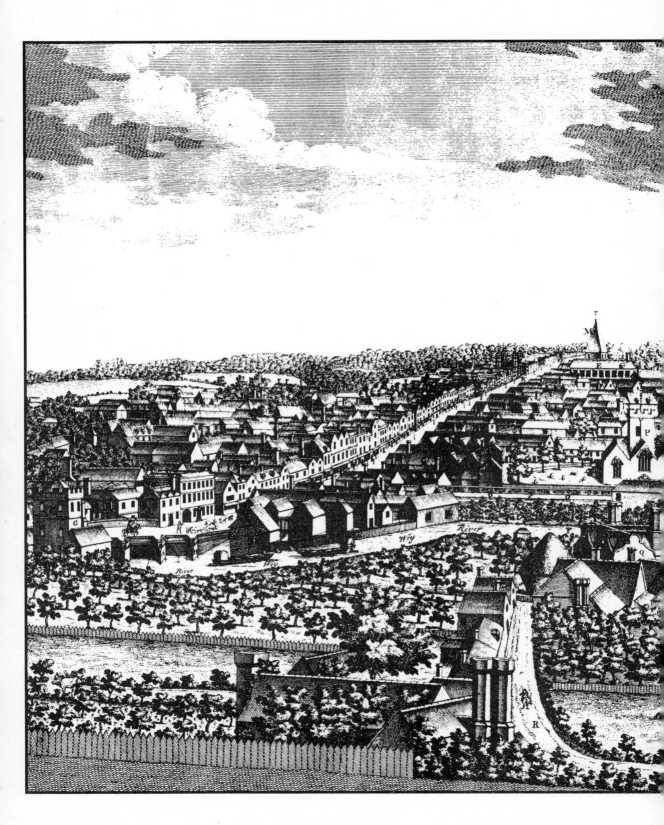